Teenage Sexuality

Teenage Sexuality
Health, Risk and Education

Edited by

John Coleman

and

Debi Roker

Trust for the Study of Adolescence
Brighton, UK

harwood academic publishers
Australia • Canada • China • France • Germany • India • Japan
Luxembourg • Malaysia • The Netherlands • Russia • Singapore
Switzerland • Thailand

Amsteldijk 166
1st Floor
1079 LH Amsterdam
The Netherlands

British Library Cataloguing in Publication Data

Teenage sexuality : health, risk and education
  1. Teenagers – Sexual behavior   2. Sex instruction for teenagers
  I. Coleman, John C. (John Christopher), 1940- II. Roker, Debi
306. 7'0835

  ISBN 90-5702-308-3   (softcover)

Contents

List of Contributors

Isobel Allen, *Policy Studies Institute, London, UK*

John Coleman, *Trust for the Study of Adolescence, Brighton, UK*

Adrian Coyle, *University of Surrey, Guildford, UK*

Janet Holland, *South Bank University, London, UK*

Alex Mellanby, *University of Exeter, UK*

Anne Mitchell, *La Trobe University, Melbourne, Australia*

Kirsti Mitchell, *London School of Hygiene and Tropical Medicine, London, UK*

Susan Moore, *Victoria University of Technology, Melbourne, Australia*

John Rees, *University of Exeter, UK*

Debi Roker, *Trust for the Study of Adolescence, Brighton, UK*

Doreen Rosenthal, *La Trobe University, Melbourne, Australia*

Rachel Thomson, *South Bank University, London, UK*

John Tripp, *University of Exeter, UK*

Kaye Wellings, *London School of Hygiene and Tropical Medicine, London, UK*

Sandra Winn, *University of Brighton, UK*

ONE

Introduction

Debi Roker and John Coleman

Teenage sexuality is a topic of considerable public and political debate, which regularly appears in the media. Consider, for example, the topics the media focus on most often — changing (and earlier) patterns of sexual intercourse amongst the young; 12 year-olds who become pregnant; parents who are grandparents at the age of 30. These sorts of stories occupy numerous pages of pictures and comment, prompt fierce debate, and appear with considerable regularity.

One effect of this type of media reporting is that it creates a sense of moral panic, implying that young people today are involved in shocking and morally reprehensible behaviour in their sexual lives. This has two effects. First, it obscures the fact that the majority of young people move into adulthood as healthy and responsible sexual beings. Second, it avoids asking the questions that we should, in fact, be addressing — such as at what age should young people be considered responsible for making decisions about their bodies and their lives, and how do we educate and support young people in their sexual development?

As well as failing to address fundamental issues such as these, the current moral panic about young people's sexual lives does little to inform and support those who work with young people. Indeed, it often serves to limit the way in which practitioners are able to work with this group. Further, although much interesting and useful research has been undertaken in the field of teenage sexuality, this is often not made accessible to those who are working with young people in a variety of settings, including the youth service, social services, health promotion, and voluntary fields. This, therefore, is the primary aim of this book — to move beyond stereotypes and media images of young people and their developing sexuality, and

1

to highlight information from the research field that is likely to be of use to those working with young people.

This chapter aims to do four things. First, there is a brief introduction to the topic of teenage sexuality, focussing on teenage sexuality as a normal part of human development and looking at the meaning of teenage sexuality for adults and society more generally. Second, there is a summary of some of the main research information available about young people and sexuality, including physical development in adolescence, patterns of adolescent sexuality, and the nature of early relationships. Third, a number of particular issues in teenage sexuality are highlighted. Many of these, such as gender issues, the development of sexual orientation, sexual risk, and education and information, are further explored in the chapters that follow. Finally, there is an outline of the areas and issues addressed in the eight chapters that follow. Comments from young people and from parents are included in the chapter, drawn from interviews undertaken by the editors with a broad range of families over the past few years.

Introduction: Teenage sexuality

In considering sexual development in adolescence, there is sometimes a tendency to believe that, before the changes of puberty, children and young people were sexually unaware and inactive. Clearly this is not the case. Rather, sexual development in the teenage years is a continuation of the development that has taken place since birth. This can be seen in a number of ways. Babies and children are almost universally curious about their own bodies, how it works, and about the bodies of others. They are interested in them, ask questions about them, and like to touch them. In particular, they are aware of themselves as a 'boy' or a 'girl', and of the different roles and expectations of the different genders. Thus a sense of sexual parts, sexual motives and sexual roles is likely to be part of a child's thinking before the bodily and emotional changes of adolescence start to occur.

Indeed, many (often quite young) children are sufficiently glued to soaps such as Neighbours and Eastenders that topics such as 'having sex', relationships, sexual attraction and desire, pregnancy, being gay and the like are fairly familiar to most. Clearly, there will be many details about these things which will be unclear, but it is further evidence that sexuality is not something which young people suddenly 'discover' in the teenage years. The issue of where and how young people acquire information about sexual matters is important, particularly in relation to television and the broader media. This issue will be returned to later in the chapter.

It is also important in this introduction, to stress that 'sexuality' is a very broad area indeed. Sometimes teenage sexuality is discussed very simplistically, and generally as the act of sexual intercourse (and in turn, generally as heterosexual intercourse). However, in talking about sexual development in the teenage years it is important to adopt a very wide remit. Thus sexual development includes the physical changes of puberty and the ability to conceive, sexual desire and emotions, crushes and fantasies, images and reputations, gossip, identities and experimentation, and changing relationships. It is often difficult for adults (and in particular for parents) to see children becoming 'sexual' in any of these ways; the broader issue of the meaning of teenage sexuality for society generally is further discussed below. Thus it is important to stress that sexual development in adolescence is much more than just the act of intercourse. Talking, for example, to any group of teenagers about their views on 'love', 'respect', 'relationships', 'reputations' and 'sex' is likely to provoke a broad ranging and varied discourse.

It was suggested above that it can often be very difficult for adults (and in particular for parents) to discuss and accept the fact that children are becoming 'sexual' in any of the ways described. There are a number of reasons for this. One of these is embarassment, with many aspects of sexuality (such as masturbation or menstruation) difficult for adults to talk about between themselves, let alone to discuss with young people. Another reason for the difficulty of communication about sexuality is that, for many adults, the topic can remind them of painful or difficult experiences in their own past. Further, adults may wish to protect young people, or feel uncertain about how to talk about some of these particularly difficult issues. It has also already been suggested that it is often difficult for parents of teenagers to accept that their child is developing sexually. This change in their children may also occur at a time when the parents' relationships are also changing.

In talking about generational issues it is of note that young people today are much more tolerant and open about many aspects of personal morality, including sexuality, than previous generations.[1] This fact no doubt heightens the anxieties of some adults. Though seeing adverts for sanitary towels on television, or two men kissing in a scene on a TV soap, may be a fairly routine occurence for many young people, it can be embarrassing and confusing for many adults, for whom such things were rarely talked about in their day. This fact is further complicated when parents have a particular religious belief, or come from a particular culture where such things are less acceptable.

At this point it is useful to consider, in more detail, what current information is available about some of the patterns of teenage sexuality, in terms of health, risk, and education.

Developing sexuality in adolescence: what research tells us

This section focusses on the actual changes that take place during the teenage years, in terms of the physical and psychological changes of puberty, changing social and peer relationships during adolescence, and patterns of sexual activity.

The changes of puberty, in terms of the physical changes, are most likely to be well known to readers of this book and are well documented.[2] What is less well known, perhaps, is the significant difference in the timing of these changes for boys and girls, and the historical changes that have occurred in the changes of puberty. In terms of gender, the average age for the onset of puberty is earlier for girls than for boys — age ten to ten-and-a-half for girls, and eleven-and-a-half to twelve for boys. The actual physical changes of puberty generally last for about two years, starting most commonly in boys with the growth spurt, and in girls with the growth of pubic hair and breasts. However, it is important to stress that there is wide variation in both the pattern and the timing of puberty (see for example Alsaker[3]).

As stated above, although the general pattern and timing of puberty is quite well known, most people are less familiar with the fact that puberty occurs much earlier now in Britain (and many other Western countries) than it did in the past. On average, puberty has started one month earlier each decade this century. Thus, for example, twenty years ago few girls would have been menstruating in the final year of primary school or in the first year of secondary school. Research shows, however, that by the first year of secondary school one in every four girls have now started menstruating.[4] The fact that children are experiencing puberty earlier is a significant development, and one which has considerable implications for education and young people's sexual behaviour.

The changes of puberty are not only physical of course. Psychologically there is a fair amount of adjustment needed, and many young people will have times when they feel confused, excited, anxious, or uncomfortable. They can also feel particularly self-conscious, and many young people need a great deal of reassurance that what is happening to them and how they feel is 'normal'. Mood swings are a perfectly normal part of puberty, and many young people need reassurance that most people feel the way they do. It is of note that research shows that those young people who are early or later developers may need extra support from those around them, particularly in relation to social relationships and the expectations of others. One young woman for example told us that:

"Well I think I probably changed a lot younger than my school-mates. And that was very embarassing... Where, you know, if I was wearing a bra all the boys would go round pinging at me, just being thoroughly annoying. And that was very embarrassing..." (16 year-old young woman)

There are a large number of books and materials available now to help children and young people think about and understand some of the things that are happening to them. These can be very useful in work with young people, especially those who are about to start or have already begun to develop (see for example publications by Stoppard[5] and Madaras[6]). There is always a danger of pathologising this aspect of development, and it is important to remember that most young people 'get through' puberty, in the sense of developing into a healthy adult. For many it is a real sign that they are moving from childhood to adulthood, and most are excited by that prospect. Central to the successful negotiation of puberty is getting good information, advice, and support; this will be discussed later in the chapter.

One consequence of puberty and the onset of the teenage years is that young people's friends and social groups change, often quite dramatically, and the nature of their close relationships alter. Girls and boys become much more aware of themselves as being part of a particular gender group, and of the roles and expectations of that group. In the early years of adolescence, most friendship groups are single sex. Later in the teenage years there is a significant change, with groups becoming more mixed, and with many young people developing close relationships and pairs start 'going out'. The issue of developing a sexual identity is part of this process. This issue is not one of simply 'being straight' or 'being gay'. Many young people will have a variety of emotions and feelings in the teenage years, including feeling attracted to those of their own gender and those of the opposite gender. For some this will lead to the development of a straight or a gay sexual identity. For others the issue will not be this straightforward — for example they may become bisexual, or be outwardly straight but also involved in gay relationships. The topic of sexual identity is discussed in detail in Adrian Coyle's chapter in this book.

The changes of puberty and sexual development will result in many young people starting personal relationships and, eventually, to having sexual relationships. There is an enormous amount of variety in the patterns of young people's sexual activity. As demonstrated above, there is a great deal of anecdotal evidence available in relation to young people's sexual behaviour, promoted in particular by the media, and described earlier. There is, however, more accurate information available from research. It is this that is briefly reviewed in the rest of this section; a number of the chapters in this book provide further information about these topics.

There is clear evidence to show that patterns of teenage sexuality have changed considerably in the last few years. This is demonstrated in particular by statistics for the average age of first heterosexual intercourse. Research shows that the average age of first sexual intercourse has declined over the past 20–30 years from age 21 to 17 for young women, and from 20 to 17 for young men.[7] Further, this research showed that one in five of those aged 16 and under were sexually active. This is clearly an important change in sexual behaviour, and is likely to be linked to a number of factors, including the availability of contraception, changing attitudes towards sexual activity in society, and the earlier age of sexual maturity described above. However, these statistics are also a challenge to the commonly expressed stereotype of the teenage years, that the majority of school-age young people are sexually active. Clearly, these figures suggest that four out of five young people have not had intercourse prior to leaving secondary school.

Patterns of sexual activity are not, however, uniform across all social and cultural groups. Wellings *et al.*[7] show that those young people from middle class families have their first experience of sexual intercourse approximately two years later than those in working class families. There is a similar link to educational level, with those in more academic trajectories likely to have first intercourse at an older age, and also, if they do become pregnant, more likely to have an abortion rather than continue with their pregnancy. Further, culture and ethnicity are important factors in sexual behaviour. Research shows, for example, that Asian young women and young men are likely to become sexually active at a later age than most other ethnic groups.

Research in this area suggests that the earlier a young person begins sexual relationships the less likely they are to use contraception. Thus one study found that 50% of 16 year-olds used no contraception the first time they had intercourse,[8] another reporting that 30–50% of teenagers did not use any contraception.[9] Reasons given included not having any contraception, being embarrassed about mentioning it, being drunk, and believing 'it wouldn't happen to me'.

There are clearly a number of implications of not using contraception. First, the possibility of conceiving is one possible outcome. One young woman described her experience of an unplanned pregnancy to us:

"I remember feeling such a fool, an idiot. They'd all said... well we just knew, all my friends and me that you couldn't get pregnant the first time. And there was me three months gone. Yeah, I felt such a idiot..."   (15 year-old young woman)

It is well documented that Britain has the highest rate of teenage pregnancy in Europe, with approximately 8,000 girls under the age of 16 becoming pregnant each year. Approximately two-thirds of this group go on to have abortions, with considerable psychological distress caused to many. The second possible outcome of not using contraception is the transmission of sexually transmitted diseases, including the HIV virus. Department of Health figures show that one in five HIV infections is among 15–24 year-olds.[10] However, many other STDs, and the cervical abnormalities associated with them, have also been shown to have increased amongst young people in recent years.[11, 12]

Finally in this section it is of note that many research studies report that many people, with hindsight, believe that they had their first sexual experience too early. The study by Wellings *et al.*[7] for example, found that a third of women aged 16–24 considered their first experience of intercourse to have been too soon. This figure rises to 50% for those who were aged under 16 at the time. It is of note that men were much less likely to express regret in this way, although it is of note that some of the young men we spoke to did have a sense of being pushed in to sexual activity before they felt ready:

"Well I was thirteen. I remember all my mates were taking the piss, saying they'd done it and that I was a wimp. I felt really bad, embarrassed. So I thought yeah I gotta do it. So I was at a party and there was this girl and we did it. I don't remember feeling much, I don't think she did either. But I thought at least I can say to me mates 'yeah of course I've done it'. Then later I found that none of them had actually done it at all. I was really pissed off." (16 year-old young man)

This gender difference is an indication of the different expectations and roles of men and women in sexual behaviour, and also the unequal power relationships inherent in this. This issue is also closely related to the negotiation of sexual activity more generally and the use of contraception in particular, indicated above. (This topic is explored in detail in the chapter by Rachel Thomson and Janet Holland).

Issues in teenage sexuality

This section of the chapter expands on some of the topics raised above, and introduces other important and topical issues in rela tion to teenage sexuality. It includes discussion of the following topics: Issues involved in researching teenage sexuality; What is sexual health?; Information and education about sexuality.

Researching youth sexuality

Researching teenage sexuality is a potentially very difficult topic, open to all sorts of misunderstandings and objections. Problems can occur at a number of levels. First, for example, there is the difficulty of getting access to young people to talk about sensitive issues. Schools are understandably wary, wanting both to protect young people from intrusion and embarrassment, and to avoid conflict with parents or governors. The youth service is also wary for the same reasons. Issues of confidentiality for schools and for young people are crucial in this respect, and have to be negotiated with care.

The second area of difficulty in terms of doing research in this area concerns the topics that are explored. In a recent piece of research into young people's knowledge about puberty and sexual development,[13] the authors were able to ask young people, anonymously in questionnaires, about a range of topics in these areas. However, we were not allowed to ask questions about sexual identity and whether or not the young people had had sexual intercourse. Clearly, this limits the issues that can be investigated within research, and the information that results from a study.

Thirdly, there are difficulties in relation to language and meaning. Consider for example the following exchange that occurred in an interview, aiming to find out whether a young women had had sexual intercourse:

Interviewer : Can you tell me whether you're sexually active?
15 year-old : Umm, no, no.
Interviewer : OK and are –
15 year-old : Well it's more –
Interviewer : Are you? Are you sexually active?
15 year-old : Well no, I'd say I'm not active really, I just lie there.

This exchange demonstrates just one way in which terminology and modes of questioning young people can produce incorrect or confusing information about sexuality. Terms are fluid and have different meanings for different individuals. In particular there are many slang words used by different groups of young people, often with very different meanings when used by young people from different cultures or who are from different parts of the country.

Fourthly, and related to the point above, there are issues around the methodologies used to investigate sexual behaviour and attitudes in adolescence. Many young people (and adults for that matter) find questions about their body and sexual lives embarrassing and awkward. This suggests that quantitative methods (such as questionnaires) might be most appropriate, in terms of ensuring anonymity. However, it is also clear that these methods do not allow young people to offer their own meanings and understandings of terms and issues, as the above quotation demonstrated very clearly. This suggests that, as with many research topics, a range of methodologies is likely to be most appropriate. However, the additional sensitivity of the issues and the need for carefully considering issues of consent and confidentiality is particularly important in research in this area.

What is sexual health?

In the introduction to this chapter, it was suggested that a conversation with young people about 'love', 'respect', 'reputations' and 'sex' would produce a fairly lively and varied discourse. Certainly, similar debates would most likely be sparked by a discussion about the nature of sexual health. Certainly, research shows that young people feel it is much more than simply the avoidance of risk or harm, which is the way in which teenage sexuality is often presented (and is one reason why the subtitle to this book is '*health*, risk and education').

Thus sexual health needs to viewed as more than just the opposite of risk and the avoidance of harm. Clearly there are risks in young people's sexual lives, including of coercion and violence, an unplanned pregnancy, and the contraction of a range of sexually transmitted diseases. However, sexuality for all age groups is clearly much more than a range of negative outcomes, and is rather a natural and generally very enjoyable part of human life. It was also one of the things that, as described above, adults can find difficult — the recognition that children are becoming sexually aware, and possibly sexually active.

Thus sexual health is a broad range of feelings, abilities, and activities, which is likely to mean different things to different people at different ages (see Reiss[14] for a discussion). However, it is likely to include the following:

- feeling comfortable and assured about the changes of puberty and the changing nature of relationships and emotions associated with these changes

- having the personal skills and the confidence to resist the pressure to have sexual relationships before the person is ready
- having respect for the needs and views of others, and for the different nature of others (for example accepting gay young people)
- feeling happy and supported in a sexual identity
- having correct information about fertility and contraception, and feeling able to use that information in personal decision-making

It is noticeable in this light that young people are not provided with very good role models about what is healthy, when they look at the personal relationships and sexual behaviours of adults in the world around them. They regularly see adults getting divorced, having affairs, and behaving inconsiderately towards others. They then hear politicians and some sections of the media condemn young people for their behaviour. Clearly, if sexual health is something to which most people aspire, then adults do not always provide good role models for young people.

In concluding this section, it is also useful to consider here the uncertain status of young people in terms of the law and their rights. This aspect is crucial to any discussion of sexual health. When are young people responsible for making their own decisions? What rights to privacy do they have? When should a young person be able to legally engage in heterosexual or homosexual relationships? How much freedom should they have, and at what age, in relation to advice about contraception for example? Society gives conflicting messages on these issues, and many young people are confused about their rights, and where they can go for information and advice. Part of being sexually healthy is feeling, for example, that you have people to talk to about fears and worries, and that you know where and how to get advice or services such as contraception. Many young people do not know, however, that they can go to their doctor for confidential advice, without their parents knowing. The Gillick case in the 1980s led to widespread confusion and uncertainty amongst many young people about their rights in this area. Thus it is important that accessible and up to date information is made available to young people on these issues. This sort of information is a key aspect of sexual health.

Information and education about sexuality

Finally in this section, consideration is given to how young people acquire information about sexual development and sexuality issues, including a consideration of the important role of the media in this.

A number of research studies have explored young people's knowledge about sexuality, and also their sources of information in this area. One study by Clark and Coleman looked at the experiences of 80 young women who became pregnant at the age of 16 and under.[15] Of this group, 60% said that they were ignorant of the facts about fertility and contraception that could have prevented their pregnancy. One recent qualitative study by Barbara Walker into young people's knowledge suggested that young people suffer an 'information famine' about sex and sexuality, with inaccurate and incorrect information passed on between peers.[16] A similar conclusion was drawn from a study of sex education classes with 465 13 and 14 year-olds.[17] This study concluded that a 'significantly large' number of this group had wrong and inaccurate information about their developing bodies and sexuality. Finally, a review of research by the Sex Education Forum led to the conclusion that:

"While young people may be more familiar with certain sexual words and phrases than their parents, for many there is a real lack of understanding of their own bodies and sexual issues" (Sex Education Forum, 1994[18])

Evidence from these and other studies thus suggests that many young people do not have sufficient information to enable them to make healthy and safe decisions. This has clear implications for young people's sexual health, as discussed earlier.

It is important, therefore, to understand the sources of young people's information about sexual matters. As the research by

Walker[16] demonstrated, much information about sexual matters is passed between young people in 'chinese whispers' style. Clearly, peers and friends are very important sources of information. However, although sometimes correct and helpful, such as:

"I remember when I first heard my friends talk about periods and I thought 'God that's gonna happen to me' and it sounded horrible. But they said.. you know that it's like becoming a woman, a sign that you're older and I thought yeah, I don't mind that so much" (13 year-old young woman)

At other times this information is incorrect and makes young people unduly anxious or uncertain. For example:

"It was my friends saying about how you can get a girl pregnant, what you do and how it happens, and I just didn't understand it, not at all, but I was too embarrassed to admit it" (15 year-old young man)

Parents are often described as those who should be the main source of information for young people on these topics. However, many young people report feeling unable or unwilling to talk to a parent about embarrassing issues such as sex and relationships (with many parents also saying the same[18]). Most parents say that they would like schools to be the main source of information for young people on sexual matters. There has certainly been a considerable change in the UK in the way in which schools inform and educate young people in this area during this century. Although provision is still very variable across the country, the majority of secondary (and most primary) schools now have a clear and agreed programme of sex education. Rather than the overtly biological approach generally adopted in the past, the majority of schools now have a broad-ranging and predominantly skills based sex education curriculum. Many areas of sex education continue to be controversial, however, including the age at which certain topics are introduced, whether and how topics such as homosexuality are included, and how aspects of gender roles and cultural/religious issues are addressed. Many of these issues are explored in the chapters that follow.

In talking about sex education and information for young people, there is also a fear amongst some politicians and policy-makers, reflected in much of the political debate that has taken place over the last few years, that talking to young people and informing them about sexual matters will encourage early sexual activity. However, there is no evidence for this. Rather, research shows the opposite — where there is good communication within the family about sexual matters, and where information is made available to them, the less likely young people are to engage in early sexual activity and the more likely they are to use contraception when they do.[19]

This does not affect, however, the difficulties that most parents face in tackling such topics with their teenagers. It is of note that a number of the parents that we interviewed talked about how, instead of broaching sexual topics in conversations, they left information about for their teenagers to read:

"I went and bought my various books at various stages, which my children found very helpful. In fact their friends didn't know quite a lot of what was in the books, and they brought them round to look at them. We've always kept the books in the sitting room, and they are there for anybody who wants to look at them at any time. I don't think anyone feels embarrassment about taking it out and reading it up"

Others told us how they used TV soaps, which parents often watched along with their teenagers, to initiate conversations about difficult issues. Parents used certain topics that arose, hoping to get their teenager to think about or discuss difficult issues that they might face in the future, such as pressure to have sex or negotiating contraception.

This brings us on to discuss of a key topic, that of the influence of the media on young people's sexual knowledge, views and understanding. The media is far more 'sexualised' now than at any time in history. Television programmes, films, newspapers, and magazines all contain stories, information, and gossip about sexual issues. This is particularly so for teenage magazines, which are avidly read by a large number of young people. Many of these magazines set the agenda, in terms of what young people should be concerned about — how to french kiss, when to say no and when to say yes, how to 'perform' well, etc. The actual effect on teenagers of these implicit (and sometimes explicit) messages is unclear. However, despite much of the negative publicity that they receive, it is also true that they provide valuable sources of information for young people, particularly in the 'agony aunt' and 'agony uncle' columns. Here, problems are discussed and concerns explored in a straightforward and unashamed manner. Many young people also comment on the value of teenage magazines because of their anonymity.

This chapter has aimed to identify and explore some of the key issues around sexuality in the teenage years. Many are large and important topics, and have only been briefly examined here. However, a number of references are given at the end of the chapter which provide useful reading and further information on these topics. Further, many of the issues are explored in more depth in the chapters to follow. The final part of this chapter outlines the topics covered in this book.

Outline of the book

The book contains eight chapters. All follow an agreed format: Reviewing the literature and information available in a particular area of teenage sexuality, discussing the author(s)' own work in this area, and considering the implications of these for those working with young people in a variety of settings.

A number of the chapters aim to explore and provide new information about areas where there has been limited understanding and debate so far. The chapter by Winn, Roker and Coleman (Chapter 2) further explores the issue of what young people know about puberty and sexual development, and the implications of this for health and sex education in schools; further, it considers some of the methodological issues, highlighted above, which are involved in trying to measure sexual knowledge. The contribution by Moore and Rosenthal (Chapter 3) considers in much greater depth some of the issues introduced above, in relation to the nature of teenage relationships and specifically sexual relationships.

In particular these authors argue for a move away from the deficit model of teenage sexuality, to a focus on the positive, life-affirming nature of this aspect of human development. Coyle (Chapter 9) explores the issue of sexual identity, moving the debate on from simplistic views to a more complex understanding of the nature of relationships and identity in the teenage years. Similarly, Thomson and Holland use information from their own research on the negotiation of heterosexual relationships to provide a clear analysis of issues of gender, roles, needs and actions.

A number of the chapters focus on different aspects of health education and information provision for young people, in a variety of different contexts. Chapter 8 (by Rees, Mellanby and Tripp) considers the issue of peer education in relation to health and sexuality, and outlines some of the issues and difficulties that need to be addressed within any such programme. The contribution by Allen (Chapter 7) considers the issues involved in providing effective contraceptive services for young people. Mitchell (Chapter 6) explores some of the implications of different approaches to work with young people around STDs and HIV/AIDS. Chapter 5 (by Wellings and Mitchell) focusses on the factors associated with pregnancy in the teenage years, and the implications of this for a young parent's life chances; it also considers the practical implications of this knowledge for work with young people.

Finally, there is a concluding chapter, written by the editors, which aims to provide a commentary and a synthesis of the main implications of the chapters for youth policy and for work with young people. A list of useful organisations working in the area of teenage sexuality is also included at the end of the book.

References

1. Halpern, D. (1995), 'Values, morals and modernity: The values, constraints and norms of European youth'. In M. Rutter and D. Smith (Eds.) *Psychosocial Disorders in Young People: Their Trends and Causes*. Chichester: Academia Europa.

2. Coleman, J.C. (1995), *Teenagers and Sexuality*. London: Hodder Headline.

3. Alsaker, F. (1996), The impact of puberty. *Journal of Child Psychology and Psychiatry*, 37: 249–258.

4. Prendergast, S. (1992), *This Is The Time To Grow Up: Girls experiences of menstruation in schools*. London: Health Promotion Research Trust.

5. Stoppard, M. (1987), *Everygirl's Life-guide*. London: Kindersley.

6. Madaras, L. (1989), *What's Happening To My Body?: A growing up guide for parents and sons*. London: Penguin.

7. Wellings, K., Field, J., Johnson, A.M. and Wadsworth, J. (1994), *National Survey of Sexual Attitudes and Lifestyles*. London: Penguin.

8. Ford, N. (1991), *The Socio-sexual Lifestyles of Young People in South-West England*. Bristol:South Western Regional Health Authority.

9. Kruss, G. (1992), *Young People and Health*. Belfast: Whiterock.

10. Department of Health (1994), *Quarterly AIDS Figures*. London: Department of Health.

11. Elliot, P.M. (1989), Changing character of cervical cancer in young women. *British Medical Journal*, 298: 288–290.

12. Donovan, C. (1990), Adolescent sexuality. *British Medical Journal*, 63: 935–941.

13. Winn, S., Roker, D. and Coleman, J. C. (1995), Knowledge about puberty and sexual development in 11–16 year-olds: Implications for health and sex education in schools. *Educational Studies*, 21: 187–201.

14. Reiss, M. (1993), What are the aims of school sex education? *Cambridge Journal of Education*, 23: 125–126.

15. Clark, E. and Coleman, J.C. (1992), *Growing Up Fast*. London: St Michael's Fellowship.

16. Walker, B. (1994), '*No one to talk with*' *Norfolk Young People's Conversations About Sex*. University of East Anglia: Centre for Applied Research in Education.

17. Phelps, F., Mellanby, A. and Tripp, J. (1992), So you think you really understand sex? *Education and Health*, 10: 27–31.

18. Sex Education Forum (1994), *Highlight No. 128: Sex Education*. London: National Children's Bureau.

19. Wellings, K. (1996), *Teenage sexuality, fertility and life chances*. Report for the Department of Health.

TWO

Young People's Sexual Knowledge

Sandra Winn, Debi Roker and John Coleman

" I remember feeling such a fool, an idiot. They'd all said... well we just knew, all my friends and me that you couldn't get pregnant the first time. And there was me three months gone. Yeah, I felt such a idiot..." (15 year-old young woman)

This chapter looks at what young people know about puberty, sexuality and sexual development, and the implications of this knowledge for the sexual health of teenagers.

Looking at what young people know about sexual matters is unfashionable to say the least — recently the main focus of sexual health education has been on the development of personal skills, communication issues, and on actual behaviour. However, although this change of emphasis is to be welcomed, this chapter aims to show that what young people know about the changes of puberty and sexual issues is also a crucial part of sexual health, with clear implications for sexual behaviour, risks, and outcomes.

The chapter will review some of main literature in this area, and suggest why a renewed emphasis on knowledge is justified. Quotes from young people are included to illustrate some of the points made. Research undertaken by the authors will be described, which explored knowledge about puberty and sex in a sample of 737 11–16 year-olds. This research made some important findings with regard to areas of high and low knowledge, and also about age-related trends in knowledge and gender differences. The implications of these results for health and sex education with young people are also discussed.

Introduction: Does knowledge matter?

Sexual knowledge is often neglected by researchers and professionals (with the notable exception of work by Goldman and

Goldman[1]). This neglect is mainly a result of the poor correlation between knowledge and behaviour, and because of the fear of reducing sexuality to a series of facts. However, what young people know about puberty and sexual development is, we believe, vitally important for healthy development during adolescence. It is an essential addition to the focus in current sex education on skills, attitudes, and communication.

We would suggest that there are four reasons for focussing on knowledge: First, knowledge is crucial for psychological adjustment during adolescence. Clearly, knowing what is likely to happen to your body makes adjusting to the changes that occur that much easier. It has been shown for example that a girl's knowledge about menstruation before her periods start makes a significant contribution to her later psychological adjustment to the changes of puberty.[2] This is particularly important in light of findings (already detailed in Chapter 1) that puberty is occurring earlier than in previous generations. Thus one in four girls will have started menstruating by the first year of secondary school, i.e. age 11–12.[3]

Second, knowledge is a pre-requisite for safe behaviour. Clearly, young people must know about how to protect themselves if they are to keep themselves safe. Knowledge may often, of course, not make a difference to behaviour. A sexually active young woman, for example, may know about the need to use contraception but still not use any. Another sexually active young woman, who is unaware of the facts about conception, fertility and STDs, will be unable to protect herself — the 15 year-old young woman quoted at the start of this chapter demonstrates this well. Another example of this is a study by Clark and Coleman of 80 young women who became pregnant at the age of 16 and under. This found that 60% were ignorant of the facts about fertility and contraception that could have prevented their unplanned pregnancy.[4] Young people's knowledge is particularly important in light of the fact, demonstrated in Chapter 1, that the majority of young people are now having sexual intercourse at a younger age than in previous generations.[5, 6] Also, as was shown in that chapter, lack of knowledge can have serious consequences in terms of the risks of an un-planned pregnancy and sexually transmitted diseases.

Third, understanding what young people know about puberty and sexual development is essential for the design and evaluation of sex education programmes in schools. To ensure that an educational programme achieves its aims, an assessment of knowledge needs to be made before and after teaching. Effective sex education can only be undertaken if there is a method of evaluating where young people are at the start of the programme, and the outcomes of that programme. Knowledge must necessarily be one outcome measured as part of such an evaluation.

Fourthly, knowledge is important because it enables young people to know what is actually happening in the world of teenage sex. For example, it is known that many young people feel they should have sex at an early age because "all their friends have".[7] However, with the average age of first sexual intercourse being 17, it is unlikely that this is the case. Having accurate information about the possibly exaggerated nature of sexual talk, and the nature of sexual reputations, may enable young people to act as they wish rather than follow what they think is happening around them. The following quote from a 16 year-old young man, talking about his first experience of sexual intercourse, demonstrates this clearly:

"Well I was thirteen. I remember all my mates were taking the piss, saying they'd done it and that I was a wimp. I felt really bad, embarrassed. So I thought yeah I gotta do it. So I was at a party and there was this girl and we did it. I don't remember feeling much, I don't think she did either. But I thought at least I can say to my mates 'yeah of course I've done it'. Then later I found that none of them had actually done it at all. I was really pissed off." (16 year-old young man)

It is possible that if this young man had known that most young people do not have sex at the age of 13, and that many young people exaggerate their sexual histories to maintain a certain image, then he may not have had intercourse when he did.

On the basis of these four points, it is suggested therefore that renewed attention be paid to the topic of young people's knowledge about puberty and sexual development.

Only a few researchers have looked at young people's knowledge in these areas. Generally, the picture is confused, with contradictory information about what young people know and don't know about puberty, sex and sexuality. However, a number of studies have highlighted the difficulty for young people of getting clear and accurate information on this topic. One recent study by Walker suggested that young people suffer an "information famine" about sex and sexuality, with inaccurate and incorrect information passed on between peers.[7] This study found that much information between young people is passed through a form of chinese whispers, with accurate information confused by embarassment and bravado. As two young women told us:

"...[friends were] talking about periods and that in the playground. They were saying one can last for about six months. And you were getting really confused ... I always remember being told that you got pregnant by a seed being put in a cup. That's how you got pregnant. So I got a bit confused over that, because I thought that for about two or three years..."   (16 year-old young woman)

"When I heard my friends talking, I sort of said, 'oh yeah I know that', you know what I mean? You're dying for them to say more to see if you can hear more and get a fair idea. You sort of push them to say more so you pick up bits like that."   (17 year-old young woman)

Other studies have shown that there are myths and inaccuracies circulated around between young people, and that as a result many young people have incorrect ideas about things to do with puberty and sexuality. For example a study of sex education classes with 465 13 and 14 year-olds found that a "significantly large" number of this sample had wrong and inaccurate information about their developing bodies and sexuality.[8] Further, a review of research by the Sex Education Forum led to the conclusion that

"While young people may be more familiar with certain sexual words and phrases than their parents, for many there is a real lack of understanding of their own bodies and sexual issues" (Sex Education Forum, 1994 [9]).

It is from this premise — that many young people lack the information necessary to make healthy and informed decisions — that the current study emerged. It aimed to find out about what young people know in relation to different aspects of puberty and sexual development, and how these vary by their age and their gender.

Assessing sexual knowledge

Much of the research that has looked at young people's sexual knowledge has been on a small-scale, and often qualitative methods have been used. As a consequence, there is no reliable measure available to assess what young people know about puberty and sexual development. Measuring knowledge in these areas is clearly difficult, particularly in terms of the areas of knowledge included, and the language used.

The aim of the present study was to develop a measure that could be used in the classroom to assess young people's knowledge. In developing this measure, we were interested in a particular type of knowledge. Thus the focus of the research was not on whether young people knew the precise meaning of words or understood technical terms, but on whether they had practical knowledge which they could use to prepare themselves for the changes of puberty, and to protect themselves in sexual relationships. The development of this measure and how the data were collected is detailed below.

The sexual knowledge study

A Sexual Knowledge Questionnaire (SKQ) was developed to look at young people's knowledge about six key topics. The question topics and phraseology were developed during pilot work undertaken with a range of secondary school pupils. The six topics covered were:

- puberty
- conception
- fertility
- contraception
- HIV/AIDS
- sexually transmitted diseases

The majority of the questions gave a statement and asked the young people to tick a box to indicate whether it was true or false; other questions were multiple choice. As suggested earlier, the aim was not to test young people's understanding of technical terms, but to explore their practical everyday knowledge. Thus any unclear terms were explained, or an alternative (more commonly used) word was given. For example in the section on puberty, respondents were asked to say whether the statement 'Boys usually go through puberty earlier than girls' was true or false. Similarly in the section about contraception, respondents were asked whether it is true or false that 'It is possible for a woman to get pregnant if the man withdraws his penis before orgasm'. A few questions asked respondents to write the answer in: for example one question was 'Where can young people under the age of 16 go for information without their parents knowing...?', followed by 'for information about contraception', 'to get contraception', and 'for confidential advice', with space to then write in the answers for each.

The research was carried out during 1994 in four secondary schools in the Brighton area, the schools being selected to provide catchment areas with a range of different social and economic characteristics. In each of the schools, all young people in three classes in each of Year 7 (age 11–12), Year 9 (age 13–14) and Year 11 (age 15–16) completed the questionnaire. A researcher administered the questionnaires with a teacher present. It was explained to each class that the questionnaire was not a test, and that they should leave blank any questions to which they did not know the answer. The anonymity of the questionnaire was also stressed. In total, 737 young people aged 11–16 participated in the survey.

Results from the study

A wide variety of information was collected in the study. This part of the chapter gives the main results, by age and gender. In terms of age, it was found that total levels of knowledge increased considerably over the age range studied. In the youngest group (age 11–12), on average the respondents gave correct responses to just over half of the questions. By age 13–14, this had risen to over two-thirds, and at age 15–16 three-quarters of the questions were answered correctly.

In every age group, young people's knowledge varied between the topics covered. The 11–12 year-olds knew more about the changes that take place during puberty than about any of the other topics, with just over two-thirds of questions on this subject being answered correctly. This youngest group knew relatively little about sexually transmitted diseases other than HIV/AIDS, getting just over a third of these questions right on average. The same pattern held in the middle age group, the 13–14 year-olds. Puberty remained the topic about which young people knew most, with more than three-quarters of these questions being answered correctly by this age group. STDs other than HIV/AIDS continued to be the area about which least was known, although the proportion of correct answers given in this section of the questionnaire had risen to just over half. Among the other topics, young people's knowledge about conception and HIV/AIDS was considerably greater than their knowledge about fertility and contraception at both ages 11–12 and 13–14.

The topic about which young people's knowledge increased most between ages 11–12 and 15–16 was STDs other than HIV/AIDS, so that in the oldest group, the average proportion of correct answers in this section of the questionnaire was just over 70 per cent. By age 15–16, the differences between topics in levels of knowledge had changed. In the oldest group, the topic for which the largest number of correct answers was given was about HIV/AIDS, with fertility and contraception the topics about which the respondents knew least. At age 15–16, nearly 90% of questions about HIV/AIDS were answered correctly, compared with around 70% of questions about contraception and two-thirds of questions about fertility.

Responses to the questions were also investigated for gender differences. It was found that, at every age, girls knew more than boys. Girls also knew more than boys about almost every topic. The only areas about which boys knew slightly more than girls were puberty and STDs other than HIV/AIDS, and for the latter topic the lead of boys over girls only held until age 13–14. Girls not only knew more than boys but their knowledge also increased more between ages 11–12 and 15–16. This means that while the knowledge gap between girls and boys was small in the youngest group, with girls just marginally ahead of boys, by age 15–16 the gender gap in knowledge was quite large. In the oldest age group the difference in knowledge between boys and girls was greatest for questions about fertility, followed by contraception and STDs other than HIV/AIDS.

There were some significant gaps in young people's knowledge. For example more than half of the young people did not know that 'A condom might not work as well as it should if certain oil-based lubricants are used with it'. Even in the 15–16 age group, more than a quarter answered this question wrongly. Similarly, three-quarters of the young people believed that 'It is necessary for a man to have an orgasm (to come) in order to get a woman pregnant', and there was very little increase with age in the proportion of correct answers to this question. Significantly, nearly half of the respondents were not able to name a place 'Where young people can go to get contraception without their parents knowing'. While the proportion who did not know this decreased with age, in the oldest group 12% of respondents could not answer this question. The proportions who did not know where they could get confidential advice about sexual matters was very similar.

Finally, analyses were undertaken to explore for any differences by the school that the respondent attended. Overall, there were few differences between the results for those attending the four schools. The one significant difference between the schools was that whereas for three of the schools the greatest increase in knowledge levels was between the ages of 11–12 and 13–14, in one of the schools the greatest increase was between the ages of

13–14 and 15–16. Possible explanations for these differences are given in the section that follows.

Explaining the results

There are a number of important results from this study, many with key implications for young people's health and sex education. This section identifies some of the most significant results and discusses the broader implications of them, in particular for those who work with young people. The results demonstrated the importance of knowledge, and how it varies by gender, age, and school attended. Possible explanations for these results are given below.

The results showed a number of differences in knowledge about puberty and sexual development by age. The overall increase in knowledge with age is not surprising, in that young people's cognitive abilities and general knowledge will develop considerably between the ages of 11 and 16. Knowledge about puberty and sexual development is also likely to increase as young people discuss their changing bodies and developing sexuality informally amongst the peer group, and more formally in school sex education classes. A more surprising result was the greater increase in knowledge amongst the majority of the sample between ages 11–12 and 13–14 than between ages 13–14 and 15–16. There are a number of possible explanations for this. First, as young people begin to mature physically they become more aware of how the body works; issues such as menstruation and contraception start to have personal relevance. Second, many young people will begin to talk to friends and/or parents about their changing bodies and developing sexuality; a development in knowledge at this time is therefore likely to result. Third, most schools will start formal teaching about puberty and sexual development at this age, which will lead to an increase in knowledge. It is interesting to note that knowledge in one area — about STDs other than HIV/AIDS — increased most between ages 13–14 and 15–16. The later development of knowledge about other STDs could be explained by the more recent emergence of HIV/AIDS and the publicity and health education campaigns surrounding it.

The study also found differences in knowledge about puberty and sexual development by gender. The gender differences reported in the study were similar to those found by some other researchers (such as Kraft[10]). The differences found are likely to reflect the earlier physical and cognitive development of girls. However, it is also likely to be associated with the fact that some of the specific risks of a lack of knowledge, such as an unplanned pregnancy, affect girls directly.

Finally, few differences were found in the study between young people at the four schools which participated in the research. There are a number of possible explanations for this. One is that young people develop knowledge about their bodies at a fairly similar rate, gathering information from parents, the peer group, and the media, and relatively independently of what is taught in school. A second possibility is that the sex education programmes of the four schools were sufficiently similar for pupils to acquire knowledge at the same rate. The one puzzling result with regard to school effects is that whereas pupils at three of the schools showed the greatest increase in knowledge between ages 11–12 and 13–14, the fourth school showed the greatest increase between ages 13–14 and 15–16. The reason for this is unclear. Two possibilities are that the pupils at the fourth school have a lower general cognitive ability and so develop knowledge later than those at the other schools, or that there is a different programme of sex education at the school.

Implications for sex and health education with young people

The results reported in this study have a number of implications for health and sex education, and for helping young people to reduce their exposure to risk. In presenting the results in this chapter, we have mainly focussed on what young people know about puberty and sexual development. However, the results also demonstrate that many of the young people were ignorant of key facts about their bodies and their developing sexuality.

The results for young people's knowledge about contraception demonstrate this well. These results showed that at age 11–12 the respondents were getting about one half of the questions about contraception wrong. At this age, such a lack of knowledge is not of too great a concern. However, by age 15–16 — when some of this age group are likely to be sexually active[5] — most were still getting one in four of the questions wrong. Thus, for example, many of this age group did not know that using oil-based lubricants can affect the effectiveness of a condom, that the pill is the most effective method of contraception, and that a woman can still get pregnant if she has sex standing up. In considering the results presented in this chapter therefore, it is important to consider the implications of ignorance or having incorrect information. The consequences could well be HIV infection or an unplanned pregnancy.

The research presented here has a number of implications for sex education in schools. Three of these are particularly significant: First, it is clear that by age 15–16, when many of this age group may be sexually active,[5] a considerable number lack the information that they need in order to act safely and have healthy sexual development. Thus the study showed, for example, that most of the young people in the study had a high level of knowledge about HIV/AIDS, but less accurate knowledge about such things as fertility and contraception. This information is essential, however, if young people are to avoid such risks as being affected by an STD or an unplanned pregnancy (see for example Elliot[11] and Donovan[12]). It is possible that teaching about the risks of HIV/AIDS has dominated much sex and health education in schools, to the detriment of other equally crucial areas.

Second, the study has implications for how the needs of boys and girls are addressed in sex education. The results showed that girls have a greater knowledge than boys in all areas. It is important that boys are not left behind in learning about puberty and sexual development. This information is important for boys so that they can protect themselves from risks such as STDs and HIV/AIDS, and also so that they can be fully involved in decisions about contraception when they become sexually active. The results from this study suggest that boys and girls may need to be taught separately, in order for boys to catch up, and to enable the different needs of each gender to be addressed.

Third, the results of this study have implications for the design, content and teaching of sex education programmes. The study has shown that young people know more about some aspects of puberty and sexual development than others, and that there are particular times when knowledge develops most rapidly. Giving teachers this information could help them to target areas of particular ignorance, or young people at particular risk. Further, the Sexual Knowledge Questionnaire developed in this research is a useful and reliable measure of knowledge in this area, and is straightforward to score and to analyse. As such, it has considerable potential for use in the classroom.

A number of important questions are raised by the research, and a number of limitations were evident which need to be addressed by future research in this area. The study was limited by the range of schools included, which included very few young people from ethnic minorities. Further, because of objections from the schools, it was not possible to include questions about sexual identity in the questionnaire, or about sensitive issues such as masturbation. It was also not possible to ask the respondents whether or not they were sexually active, which meant that we could not explore the levels of knowledge of those who were and were not sexually active. Future research needs to address these areas.

Finally, it is important that we better understand the link between young people's knowledge and behaviour. In the early part of this chapter we suggest that knowledge does have a crucial link with young people's health and their behaviour. There is evidence that providing young people with information through sex education classes both reduces the age at which they start to have sexual relationships, and increases the likelihood that they will use contraception when they do. This suggests that knowledge does have a clear part to play in promoting healthy sexual behaviour during adolescence. Further research is needed in order that we better understand the relationships between young people's knowledge, attitudes and behaviours.

References

1. Goldman, R. and Goldman, J. (1982), *Children's Sexual Thinking*. London: Routledge and Kegan Paul.

2. Brooks-Gunn, J. and Reiter, E.O. (1990), The role of pubertal processes in the early adolescent transition. In S. Feldman and G. Elliot (Eds.) *At the Threshold; The Developing Adolescent.* Cambridge: Harvard University Press.

3. Prendergast, S. (1992), *This is the time to grow up: Girls experiences of menstruation in schools*. London: Health Promotion Research Trust.

4. Clark, E. and Coleman, J.C. (1992), *Growing Up Fast*. London: St. Michael's Fellowship.

5. Kruss, G. (1992), *Young People and Health*. Belfast: Whiterock.

6. Wellings, K., Field, J., Johnson, A.M. and Wadsworth, J. (1994), *National Survey of Sexual Attitudes and Lifestyles*. London: Penguin.

7. Walker, B. (1994), *"No-one to talk with": Norfolk young people's conversations about sex – a basis for peer education*. University of East Anglia: Centre for Applied Research in Education.

8. Phelps, F., Mellanby, A. and Tripp, J. (1992), So you think you really understand sex? *Education and Health*, 10. 27–31.

9. Sex Education Forum (1994), *Highlight No. 128: Sex Education*. London: National Children's Bureau.

10. Kraft, P. (1993), Sexual knowledge among Norwegian adolescents. *Journal of Adolescence*, 16: 3–21.

11. Elliot, P.M. (1989), Changing character of cervical cancer in young women. *British Medical Journal*, 298: 288–290.

12. Donovan, C. (1990), Adolescent sexuality. *British Medical Journal*, 63: 935–941.

THREE

Adolescent Sexual Behaviour

Susan Moore and Doreen Rosenthal

Orientation of the chapter

Much of the research on adolescent sexuality emphasises the problematic aspects of this phenomenon. Adolescent sexual behaviour has been linked with undesirable activities such as smoking, drug-taking, and delinquency, investigated from the framework of contraceptive inadequacies and teenage pregnancy or, more recently, explored in relation to unsafe practice and HIV risk. In this chapter, we do not want to emphasise only these 'deviant' aspects of adolescent sexuality. There is no doubt that youths' sexual behaviour can involve high risk — the emotional risks of being hurt or of developing anti-social attitudes to sexual behaviour, the physical risk of disease, especially HIV/AIDS, and the social risks of peer rejection, or of curtailing life's possibilities through unplanned parenthood. Perhaps some would add to this list the spiritual or moral risks of not following some code of behaviour. Rather than buy into this argument, we acknowledge that there are many codes of sexual behaviour consistent with social harmony and individual fulfilment. One of the tasks of adolescent/youth development is, indeed, to make commitments with respect to some such code, in other words, to develop sexual values which guide behaviour. This can be a positive, life-affirming task, along with many of the other features of sexual development. Adolescent sexual behaviour is about learning to cope with changing bodies and changing feelings, it is about the search for identity, about learning to relate to others in an intimate way, about pleasure and desire, and about becoming a mature and fully rounded person.

The communication of mixed messages about sex from the adult generation make handling sexuality a difficult but exciting challenge for adolescents. Parents, school-based sex education programs, religious institutions, peers, and media images of sex can draw adolescents in different directions, with some of these influences espousing high levels of sexual caution and conservatism, and others pushing in the direction of experience, risk-taking and variety. How young people respond to the challenge of integrating these influences, in terms of their behaviours and attitudes, is the focus of this chapter.

The role of puberty in sexual behaviour and development

Adolescent sexual behaviour is inextricably linked with the events of puberty, in which the adolescent's body develops its adult shape and capacity for reproductive functioning, and the hormonal changes affect sex drives in complex ways. Biological development does not tell the whole story of what motivates and directs adolescent sexual behaviour, because social and cultural factors also exert a strong influence on how a young person will express his or her sexuality. Nevertheless puberty provides the signal to the outside world that the child is now physically, if not emotionally, a man or a woman, and it provides all sorts of internal and external signals to the child that here are changes, urges, and feelings to be coped with, expressed, or contained.

Sexual maturation for girls includes the growth of pubic and axillary hair, breast development, and menarche, the onset of menstruation, occurring usually between 10 and 16 with a mean age for American and British populations of around 12.5 years. The menstrual cycle introduces a pattern of hormonal variations associated with ovulation, building up of the uterine lining in preparation for fertilisation, and the shedding of this lining via the menstrual period. Oestrogen and progesterone levels rise and fall in association with these events. The uterus, vagina, vulva, clitoris and other internal structures undergo growth and development so that the adolescent girl has a functional reproductive system about 12 to 18 months after the first menstrual period, and is physically capable of bearing children.

Sexual maturation for boys involves increased growth of the testes, scrotum and penis, pubic, bodily and facial hair development, and maturation of the internal prostate gland and the seminal vesicles. The first ejaculation of seminal fluid is likely to occur about 2 years after the beginning of pubic hair growth, either as a spontaneous emission or the result of masturbation. The number and mobility of sperm present in the seminal fluid increase throughout puberty, with a corresponding increase in fertility. Other changes include an increase in the size of the larynx, leading to the voice changing to deeper register, and for males and females alike, growth of the sweat glands with accompanying increases in body odour, and enlargement of the pores on facial skin, which, accompanied by hormonal changes leads to the increased likelihood of acne.[1]

With these changes come effects on mood, so that the adolescent can fluctuate between the depths of despair and the heights of elation, overwhelming confidence and morose self-doubt, affection for parents and disdain for them. In addition, libido or sexual drives develop in ways that are little understood, yet we know that young people can experience these drives in ways varying from overwhelming and frustrating to surprising and pleasant, from frightening to welcome. For young people who suspect or are sure they are gay or lesbian, these drives can be even more confusing, being seen as at odds with the prevailing cultural and peer norms. The peer group can in turn be quite malevolent in homing in on differences and rejecting or isolating the 'different' (for whatever reason) young person, at a time when peer support is so much needed. Adolescent views about what constitutes unacceptable difference can be hard for adults to fathom, varying as they do between subgroups and over time. Particular body shapes, styles of clothing or modes of behaviour ranging from the trivial, such as hairstyle, to the more substantive, like sexual orientation are all grist to the mill of adolescent anxieties about conformity. Thus physical changes within the context of social pressures will act together to influence the direction of young people's sexual behaviours and attitudes.

More wide-spread social mythologies, such as the belief that boys cannot control their sex drives but girls can, also have implications for adolescent sexual behaviour. Boys may feel they have the right to coerce girls into sexual activity, or that activities such as kissing and fondling imply permission for intercourse. Girls may feel concerns about their reputations if they are judged by peers as 'leading boys on', or they may worry that their relationships with boyfriends will be jeopardised if they do not agree to 'go all the way'. The following quotes from 16-year-olds, the first from a young man and the second from a young woman illustrate what are typical (but not universal) views about the male sex drive:[2]

1. Can boys control their sexual urges?

    "No, if you don't get a girl you go home and have a good old wank. That's why we hate cockteasers so much."

    It is often said that men are controlled by their dicks — is this true?

    "Bloody oath mate, it can make you do irrational things."

    What are women ruled by?

    "Silly, stupid, romantic notions."

2. Can boys control their sexual urges?

    "Not really, no. They can be controlled by the girl, but they certainly wouldn't stop if they wanted something. Or they might if they cared about the girl and everything."

    Can women control their sexual urges?

    "Yes"

    It is often said that men are ruled by their dicks — is this true?

    "Some are — that is all they think about. Even though they might have morals against it, because they want it so bad they will just go for it."

In terms of sexual behaviour, an increase in sexual drive does not necessarily mean that sexual activity will begin. Social factors play a large role here with studies suggesting that girls more than boys are influenced by their friends' behaviours. Girls whose best friends have had intercourse are more likely to also have had intercourse, while for boys, hormone concentration seems a more powerful indicator of sexual experience.[3] Cultural and subgroup differences in age of first intercourse are great, as will be discussed in a later section. Physical attractiveness and opportunity are also relevant factors here, for example girls who look more mature are more likely to have had intercourse than less mature looking girls, regardless of actual pubertal status.[3] Further, parental behaviours such as lower levels of parental supervision, coupled with high possibilities for interacting with the opposite sex, provide more opportunities for sexual experimentation among teenagers. Such parenting styles, while they may be associated with higher independence and social competence among teenagers, are also likely to be associated with more sexual experience.

In some cultures, puberty is marked by initiation ceremonies, completion of which confers adult status on the initiate. The protracted Western version of adolescence accords puberty little attention, with adult status dependent more on capacity to live independently from parents and be financially self sufficient. These milestones are a long way distant from puberty for most young people, and for some virtually unattainable, so that adult status must be gained in other ways, some of which have turned out to be antisocial. It has been suggested that sexual initiation has become the *rite de passage* of modern adolescents. The question that must be asked of the adult society is whether such a transition to adult status can be accepted as a normal event or whether it is defined as deviant. The answer to such as question is far from simple, involving as it does a social definition of how young is 'too young', of what is appropriate and inappropriate in sexual behaviours and their preliminaries, and of what are 'approved' freedoms and responsibilities for adolescents through the age ranges from early puberty to the late teens. In the next section we will consider the course of sexual initiation, from the gleam in the eye, as it were, through to intercourse. The 'typical' age and range of ages at which these behaviours occur will be described, an exercise which underscores the diversity rather than the conformity in Western adolescents' sexual behaviours and perceived norms.

What counts as sexual behaviour?

Autoerotic or solitary sexual behaviour includes sexual fantasies, nocturnal emission, and masturbation, subjects about which there is little research, especially among adolescents, perhaps because they are regarded as very private and even shameful activities. Thinking and dreaming about sex and sexual relationships, reading about these issues, watching them on films and videos, talking about them with others, and discovering something about the sexual responsiveness and sensuality of one's own body are all, however, part of the developmental process. These are not processes that begin abruptly at adolescence. It is part of normal childhood to discover one's body, to feel sensual pleasure, and to experience caring and being cared for — all elements of adult sexual experience. Of course it is also part of normal childhood for children to be protected from experiences that are beyond their physical and emotional capabilities, such as direct sexual overtures and expressions from others. What happens at adolescence is that the young person begins to express sexual needs of a more direct nature than in childhood — and here we are not talking necessarily about intercourse, but of experiences such as more social interaction with the opposite sex, more chance to learn about and discuss sexual issues, and a greater need for physical sexual expression of some kind. Correspondingly, the adult generation gradually removes the protections offered to children against too early sexual expression, the pace at which this occurs depending on cultural and social norms. Interestingly, although there are fewer taboos on masturbation than there once were, this is still an area about which many adults feel very uncomfortable. It may be more difficult for young people to get advice or share their concerns about this area than about the more social elements of sexual development.

In a study of 436 suburban Australian schoolchildren aged between 15 and 18 years, more boys than girls reported ever having masturbated (59 versus 43 per cent). Boys were also more likely to report masturbating more than three times a week (38 versus 9 per cent). Whether or not sexual intercourse replaced or supplemented masturbation as a sexual practice could not be resolved by the study, but there was evidence that masturbation was positively correlated with sexual self-esteem. Young people from families in which sex was perceived as more openly discussed were also more likely to self-report masturbation.[4]

While it may be difficult for young people to discuss masturbation, advice available about the social elements of sexual behaviour seems limitless. If all the books written about dating, courtship, crushes, romance, going steady, and falling in love could be recycled into energy we could probably fuel the planet for a very long time. Yet every generation of young people seems needy in this domain — each adolescent has to work out what is best for him or her in terms of development of sexual relationships and the issues of how fast, how far, and with whom. Listening to teenage girls on the telephone discuss for an hour who held whose hand at a party underscores the universal adolescent fascination with burgeoning sexuality.

It is worth remembering that the social elements of sexual expression comprise much more than the usual focus of texts on sexuality, that is, intercourse. They range from flirtation through hand-holding, kissing, fondling, mutual masturbation through to various forms of penetrative sexual encounter. A recent study of adolescent sexual timetables[5] indicated that almost all the 522 young people (15- and 16-year-olds) sampled believed that somewhere between 12 to 14 years was an appropriate age to begin 'brief' kissing on the mouth, with around 65 per cent also considering tongue kissing to be 'OK' at that age, but the rest preferring to wait until later (predominantly 15 to 17 years). Touching a girl's breasts or genitals beneath her clothes, or a boy's genitals beneath his clothes were viewed as suitable for 15 to 17 year-olds by about 70 per cent of the sample, with small minorities perceiving it as reasonable earlier or not until much later (over 21). Views about the appropriate age for intercourse were less consistent. Over half the sample thought that some time between 15 and 17 years was a reasonable age for intercourse to occur, but most of the rest nominated later ages. The study underscores the strong norms present among teenagers with respect to their sexual developmental timetables.

The pressure of these norms, and our current social obsession with intercourse can leave young people in the lurch when it comes to learning about sexual preliminaries. They can feel rushed into intercourse before they have had time to savour these other forms of sexual communication. Pre-sexual communication styles and patterns are likely to be reflected in how young people initiate and sustain their intimate, romantic, and sexual relationships. The issue of whether these three types of relationships converge into one or stay separate is just one example of how complex is the web of attitudes, skills, opportunities, and cultural pressures which influence sexual behaviour. Some young people prefer to experiment sexually without commitment, others seek to fall in love and develop intimacy, with sexual behaviour forming one aspect of that intimacy. The young person's ideal in these matters may not necessarily be attained however, as sexual expression and its concomitants depends not only on individual desires, but on the co-operation of another who shares similar desires. To find co-operative others in the joint venture of sexual expression involves social skills, the ability to communicate, the ability to be attractive at some level to the other person. Popular and classical literature attests to the fact that this venture can be fraught with disappointment, betrayal, unrequited love, deception, and miscommunication.

The research on adolescent social skills suggests that young people who are most successful in forming friendship relationships with same-sex peers will be those who have greatest success with romantic and sexually-based relationships.[6] As teenage girls' friendships are characterised by more self-disclosure, discussion of problems, sharing of emotions, and mutual support than boys' friendships, girls may have a head start on boys with respect to the more intimate aspects of romantic and sexual relationships.[7] They may be confused by boys' unpreparedness or unwillingness to express closeness through talk (rather than action). Indeed, miscommunications between the sexes about sexual and intimacy needs are common in adulthood, so it is not surprising that such communications are difficult in adolescence as well. Despite these difficulties however, most young people are motivated toward exploration of their own sexuality through relationships with others, and this motivation can be the basis of positive learning and understanding of self and others.

Falling in love

Adolescence and falling in love seem to go hand in hand. One common developmental path is that the hero worship and crushes of the early teenage years are followed by a 'real' love object, in which partners share a romantic vision of their relationship, as in these quotes from 16-year-old girls.

What do the words romantic love mean to you?

"That means to me I think losing a grip on reality, changing your perception of something, and all the world is wonderful, and you are blind to the other person's faults. It is like you acknowledge them (the faults) but they don't exist.
I would say that is someone who really cares for somebody, you actually love somebody and you sleep with them because you are really close."

A major theorist in the field of adolescent development, Erik Erikson,[8] argues that adolescent falling in love is part of the quest for identity or self-definition, whereby the young person sees an idealised version of him- or herself reflected through the eyes of another. The process is conceptualised as something akin to looking in a very flattering mirror.

"To a considerable extent, adolescent love is an attempt to arrive at a definition of one's identity by projecting one's diffused self-image on another and by seeing it thus reflected and gradually clarified. That is why so much young love is conversation."[8]

Falling in love is thus part of the process of growing up, and discovering oneself and one's sexuality. It is best seen as important for these reasons rather than as a basis for permanent commitment, according to Erikson. Making such commitments too early may limit self development and eventual maturity, unless the couple can 'grow together'. This view of adolescence as a 'moratorium' in which the young person can experiment with roles and relationships as a precursor to the more permanent love and work commitments of adulthood is popular today in western societies. Such a view enables a more benign acceptance of adolescent sexual experimentation than was once possible or, indeed, is currently possible in more sexually traditional cultures and sub-groups.

There is no doubt that ideas of love and romance are popular with young people, and that the more open and explicit sexual expression of today's youth is for many, set in a context of beliefs about true love and commitment. Loving, caring and affection were the primary motivations for having sex among the majority of the middle class samples of adolescents we have interviewed.[1] Most approved of and idealised romance and love, as in the following:

"I see romantic as roses, candlelit dinners, holding hands, walking down the beach — stuff like that. Someone to talk to, to love, basically."   (16-year-old boy)

A certain percentage was more cynical however:

"Romantic love is something that doesn't last, and it is more a dream than a reality. When you are in a romantic situation like that you are relying on your fantasies and dreams, and you are making up all these things that you think are happening, but they are not really – you just want them to happen."   (16-year-old homeless girl)

"Going all the way"

Sexual intercourse can be seen as a milestone, or even the climax, of sexual behavioural development. All societies share the hope for their young people that this event will take place at a point in their lives that is not inimical to healthy development. Nevertheless, this is an area in which we see significant cultural differences as well as historical change within cultures. In some social groups the expectation is that marriage or other forms of commitment will precede intercourse. In western societies there is a growing tolerance of non-marital youthful sexual experimentation, and this tolerance has brought with it a trend toward earlier first sexual experience. Comparisons with Kinsey's early data[9,10] suggest that the average age of sexual debut has reduced for boys over the past 40 years or so, but the change is much more dramatic for girls, particularly Caucasian girls. American writers report these changes as having arisen from the more sexually permissive attitudes of the 1960s and 70s, arguing that these attitudes became popular in the mid-1970s.[11,12,13] This increased liberalism may have occurred somewhat later in Australia. An Australian Institute of Family Studies[14] survey came to the conclusion that around 60 per cent of 17-year-olds were still virgins in the early 80s, while by 1988, this percentage appears to have dropped to 40.[15]

Current data from the British 'Sexual Attitudes and Lifestyles' survey of approximately 19,000 randomly selected individuals showed the median age of first intercourse of the youngest cohort sampled (16- to 24-year-olds), to be 17 years, some four years earlier than first intercourse of the oldest cohort (55 to 59 years).[16] In Sweden, the age of initiation into sex dropped from an average of 19 years to 16 years in the past four decades. Studies emanating from the United States suggest that the majority of teenagers have had sexual intercourse by the age of 19 years. A national longitudinal survey in that country in the late 80s showed that by age 15, about 6 per cent of girls and 17 per cent of boys had experienced intercourse, these figures rising to 44 per cent and 67 per cent respectively by age 18, and to 70 and 80 per cent by age 20. In Australia, a recent national sample survey of nearly 4000 high school students indicated that approximately half the boys and girls in year 12 (17- and 18-year-olds) had sex, with this number decreasing steadily in lower age groups.[2]

Notwithstanding the above statistics, it is misleading to talk about the average age for loss of virginity. Studies from a range of countries indicate different levels of sexual experience for similarly-aged young people from different social, religious, ethnic and racial groups. For example, white American adolescents become sexually active at an older age than Afro-Americans and are less likely to be having sex than Afro-Americans across the ages 11 to 17. Mexican-American adolescents become sexually active at an older age again than their Anglo-American counterparts. A recent study comparing Australian and South African university students showed that South African respondents were significantly more likely than their Australian counterparts to engage in vaginal and anal sex with casual and regular partners, and in withdrawal with casual partners.[17] Hofferth and Hayes[13] suggest that living in an environment characterised by poor and crowded housing and serious social disorganisation, and cultural mores which valorise male virility, are important socio-cultural factors which relate to earlier sexual activity for teenagers. More liberal sexual attitudes of certain cultures are also relevant here.

A factor which works in the opposite direction is religiosity. Young people who adhere to religious values, whatever the religion, are less likely to be sexually active.[18] A recent movement in the United States, the True Love Waits campaign, advocates no sex before marriage and is apparently gaining popularity among teenagers, especially those with strong religious beliefs. The following comments from two Greek-Australian girls indicate the influence of cultural values on beliefs about losing one's virginity. What these quotes show is that while a cultural influence may be perceived as strong by young people, other factors such as peer influence and individual differences are also important in the decision whether to have sex or wait.

"I have been brought up to believe that you don't go sleeping round with people and don't get pregnant before your wedding and things like that. Different Greek parents have different views, and some don't care, but my parents do. I don't have the same freedom as Australians. I wouldn't bring a guy home until there was a commitment to an engagement or marriage.

Well, my mother thinks that if you are under 21 you are too young to have a boyfriend and you should be a virgin until you are married...... I don't think you should be a virgin until you are married unless you really want to, and as for waiting until you are 21 to have a boyfriend ... no way."

Presenting an average age for sexual 'debut' is probably not a particularly healthy thing to do, as young people will vary in their 'readiness' to cope with sexual encounters. The belief that 'nearly everyone my age has had sex already — what's wrong with me?' places the kind of pressure on sexual development that is less than optimal (but difficult to avoid). In relation to this point, McCabe and Collins[19] note the common belief among adolescents that their peers are more sexually active than is actually the case, a belief which can constitute part of the social pressure toward intercourse.

Young people themselves tend to think that the ideal age for loss of virginity 'depends on the person' (their level of maturity), and that too early a sexual debut can have damaging psychological effects. Age 15 is often cited as 'too young' by the young people we have interviewed.[2] Nevertheless the belief that first sex should wait for marriage is no longer widely held. A common view of young people today is that sex before marriage is normal as in the following quote from a 16-year-old girl:

"It's normal to have sex before marriage. No-one waits for the ring these days. That idea is so old-fashioned. No-one thinks like that any more."

Variety of sexual experience

As discussed previously, experimentation is part of the pattern of adolescent sexuality. There has been a clear generational change in the sexual 'style' of young people in terms of the wide variety of sexual behaviours in which they engage. The Sexual Attitudes and Lifestyles survey of Johnson and colleagues[16] notes that while nearly everyone in Britain has experienced vaginal intercourse by the age of 25, there are marked age differences in other practices, particularly active and receptive oral sex. Among the sexually active 16- to 24-year-olds, 79 per cent reported experiencing oral sex in the last year and 85 per cent ever, in comparison with, for example the 45- to 49-year-old cohort for whom only 30 per cent of the women and 42 per cent of the men had oral sex in the last year. As well, only half the women and two-thirds of the men over 45 had experienced oral sex in their lifetime. A range of studies across several western countries suggest that there is a significant proportion of young people now for whom the practice of oral sex precedes intercourse. For example, Newcomer and Udry,[20] in a survey of adolescents in the USA, found that 25 per cent of virgin boys and 15 per cent of virgin girls had given or received oral-genital stimulation. The average age at which it was considered appropriate for young people to have oral sex was lower than the age deemed appropriate for intercourse among the 15 and 16-year-olds in Rosenthal and Smith's[5] recent study. The reasons for this change may relate to increases in sexual information available, to increased hygiene, to changed attitudes toward sexuality and sensuality, to changes in reporting rates, or to contraceptive issues — we do not have the research to answer this question.

Oral sex is not the only practice which appears to have gained popularity among adolescents and young people. Heterosexual anal intercourse, while uncommon, is more frequent among young people who have already experienced vaginal intercourse than among any older age groups. Breakwell and Fife-Schaw[21] found rates of about 9 per cent for their 16- to 20-year-old British sample, with the rates being slightly lower (about 7 to 8 per cent) among sexually active Australian university students. Among particular sub-groups such as the homeless, rates are much higher. One concern with this practice is the heightened potential for disease transmission, particularly HIV/AIDS, if condoms are not used. Disease transmission is also possible from unprotected vaginal intercourse, and to a lesser extent, oral sex. These possibilities will be discussed in more detail in other chapters of this book. Suffice to say that although there has been considerable increase in young people's acceptance of condoms during the past decade, studies of condom *use* show that many young people still only use them inconsistently or not at all. The increase in condom use rates appears to have occurred largely because most young people now use condoms 'sometimes'.[22,23,24]

The meaning of this is complex from the point of view of adolescent sexual health. On the positive side it indicates increased exposure to condoms and the potential for improved skill in negotiating their use, at both interpersonal and purely mechanical levels. On the other hand, it indicates that protection against sexual disease is not consistent.

Number of partners, casual sex, and "one night stands"

To what extent is partner changing a feature of adolescent and young adult sexual practice? Is the stereotype of high activity among this age group borne out by the data? Again, the wide range of attitudes toward sex exhibited by young people makes it difficult to generalise about any kind of modal attitude toward multiple partnering. Several decades ago, Sorensen[25] described the patterns of 'serial monogamy' and 'sexual adventuring' characterising youth and these patterns are still current.

Serial monogamy, the most common pattern, incorporates the idea of mutual faithfulness and commitment to the current partner as if he or she were to be permanent. This is viewed by young people as a sexually conservative mode, with the majority of adolescents expecting that they will have more than one sexual partner over a lifetime, a different expectation, perhaps, than their parents had at the same age. However partnerships do not last 'until death do us part', but in reality can be quite short-term, from a few weeks or months to a few years. In addition, although within these serial relationships faithfulness is the idealised norm, it is not consistently upheld. Young people, beginning their sexual lives earlier than their parents and marrying later are likely to have more partners in a lifetime than was the norm in previous generations.

The derogatory label of 'promiscuous' is unlikely to be attached to the young serial monogamist as it is to the sexual adventurer — the young person who experiences multiple partners without espousing faithfulness or commitment. This homeless 16-year-old gives an opinion of one-night stands which is fairly common:

What do you think of one-night stands?

"They're not on. Myself, I have had one-night stands and they don't make you feel too good. I believe in sex if you love someone and that's the main thing."

Adolescent views on casual sexual encounters vary across sub-groups and individuals but are on the whole disapproving, especially if girls engage in these behaviours. Consider the views of this 15-year-old male:

What do you think about girls who sleep around?

"Probably think that they are sluts ... if I was in a girl's position I would never do that. I don't like them."

What about boys?

"Here it changes because he is classified as a stud, pretty lucky. I would think he knows how to pick up, how to control everything, you would probably say that he is cool. Boys are the stronger species — it is like if I had a daughter I wouldn't let her do such things. I would give a boy more freedom."

Johnson and colleagues' study[16] indicates that men and women in the 16 to 24 age group consistently report the greatest numbers of partners, despite these being the group with the highest proportion of respondents who have not yet experienced intercourse. Among this age group, 11 per cent of men and 3 per cent of women reported 10 or more heterosexual partners in the last five years. The researchers argue that these figures represent not only an exploration of several relationships before committing to a long term partnership (which may have also occurred for older age groups when they were in their teens and 20s), but also a genuine generational change in sexual behaviour patterns. They note the difficulties involved in gaining precise estimates of the number of partners that older people had when they were younger, but believe their evidence points to a pattern indicating that individuals now beginning their sex lives will have, on average, a substantially greater number of partners in a lifetime than did their parents.[2]

Our studies of three different ethnic groups in Australia indicated that 16 per cent of 18-year-old tertiary student Anglo-Australian males and 8 per cent of similarly aged Anglo-Australian females had 3 or more sexual partners in the last six months, although most reported no partners or only one. Subgroups differed markedly however, with 43 per cent of Greek-Australian and 30 per cent of Italian-Australian boys reporting three or more partners over the same time period.[26] In a separate study of 16-year-olds, homeless young people were significantly more sexually active than home-based adolescents, and had more partners. Homeless boys reported an average of 12, and girls an average of 7, partners in the preceding six months, with a maximum exceeding 100 for both sexes, compared with a maximum of 5 (and an average of 1 or less) for home-based youths.[27]

Multiple partnering is not an uncommon phenomenon among young people, and if not accompanied by safe sex practices, becomes a risk factor for sexually transmissible diseases, including HIV/AIDS. The issue is complicated by young people's often inconsistent views about fidelity. The likelihood of using condoms with regular or casual partners is compromised if one partner believes that the relationship is monogamous and likely to be long-lasting, yet it is clear that in sexual relationships the question of fidelity is open to misinterpretation, deception and denial.

The research suggests that while young people espouse the idea of fidelity in their serial sexual relationships, they recognise that this is an ideal that may not always be lived up to. Among the 16-year-olds interviewed by Buzwell and her colleagues[28] only about 40 per cent said that they are (or would be) always faithful to their sexual partner. Significant numbers said they tried to be but were not always successful. A 'regular partner/casual partner' distinction was common among these teenagers, who were prepared to try fidelity if they were in a long-term, but not a short-term, partnership. In a related study of older adolescents, young people were asked if they would be faithful to their partner in a *long-term relationship* and if they expected faithfulness in return. Most girls believed they would be and expected likewise of their partners (95 per cent in both cases). Most boys (86 per cent) expected their female partner to be monogamous, but only three-quarters had the same expectation of themselves. An example illustrates the point:

Are you always faithful to your partner?

"I don't think I would be because you know she will be there and that she thinks a lot of you. And if there is an opportunity for, say, a one night stand, and you like her in a physical sort of way, then I reckon most guys would be unfaithful. Because if they think they won't get caught, they know nothing will happen to their relationship."

Cochran and Mays[29] conducted a study with young unmarried college students which indicated that dating partners often lie about whether they have been faithful and how many partners they have had in the past. Of the men, 34 per cent admitted having lied about their sexual history in order to convince a potential partner to have sex. A large proportion of both men and women said they would 'censor' information about the number of sexual partners in their past when beginning a new relationship. In addition, 22 per cent of the men and 10 per cent of the women would not disclose the existence of another partner to a new partner, and over one-third of both sexes would not admit to their partner if they had been unfaithful. These researchers note that 'dishonesty is an intimate feature of dating life'. Encouraging young people to use condoms consistently in situations where they either believe that a relationship is monogamous, or wish their partner to so believe can be especially difficult. Condom use when not attached to pregnancy prevention can be interpreted as an indication of either pre-existing infection or multiple partnering, either of which may be interpreted as jeopardising the relationship.

Sexual orientation

Issues about sexual orientation may loom large at adolescence for some young people. Decisions about homosexual, bisexual, or heterosexual behaviour, identity and life style, may be made, or considered. How crucial is the adolescent experience in shaping these choices? Obviously, experimentation with same-sex sexuality can occur at any stage of life, but according to the British Lifestyle study,[16] experimentation with and adoption of the gay lifestyle is more likely to occur among younger men. For women in their study no one age group was favoured over any other in terms of having a first homosexual encounter. Johnson and colleagues note across their total sample of ages from 16 years and above that around 7 per cent of individuals admit attraction to others of the same sex with about 6 per cent of men and 3 per cent of women reporting any homosexual experience ever. Smith and Rosenthal's[30] sample of 885 15- to 18-year-old school children in Melbourne, Australia indicated similar levels of same sex attraction as the British survey, although girls were more likely to admit such attraction than boys (11 per cent versus 6 per cent). Homosexual experimentation is not uncommon in adolescence, and does not necessarily lead to homosexual orientation in adulthood. On the other hand, homosexual attractions and fantasies occurring among young people may not be acted upon until later in life, when they feel more confident to challenge social norms. Part of the task of sexual development for young people is to consider their sexual orientation, to experiment with it mentally if not behaviourally. Homophobic societies and social groups limit this potential for experimentation and questioning to the detriment of youth. For example, in a study of adolescents from small rural towns in Australia, the level of expressed homophobia was exceptionally high, yet a significant number of young people indicated a lack of certainty about their sexual orientation (6 per cent) or were attracted to people of the same sex (5 per cent).[31] The authors comment on the anxieties and stresses which these young people experience, and the difficulties they face in receiving advice, information, and support. Homophobia also mitigates against ensuring safe sex practice in homosexual encounters, as these practices may be shrouded in secrecy, guilt, and denial. As such, planning to use condoms and carrying out those plans are less likely to occur. This creates an issue of concern particularly in western nations where HIV infection rates are higher among male homosexuals than other groups.

Summary

In short, adolescence is a time of experimentation, and sexual experimentation forms part of that exploration of new roles and new ways of behaving necessary in the formation of adult identity. Sexual relationships provide for many young people today an opportunity to move to adult roles that are substantially delayed for them in other areas, such as career choice and economic independence. While there are large between-group differences, the norm for young people appears to be approval of pre-marital sex, with loss of virginity occurring in the late teens, along with the recognition of the harmfulness of entering the sexual arena before one is 'ready'. Casual sex is more accepted for teenage boys than for teenage girls, while both sexes value love, romance, and commitment in relationships, but do not always live up to their own ideals. Social attitudes to teenage sex have softened, so that young people are more readily able to access clear information to aid them in their sexual decision-making. Given the potential for both harm and joy provided by sexual behaviour, it is important that the adult generation maintains for young people these open lines of communication about sex.

References

1. Moore, S.M. and Rosenthal, D.A. *Sexuality in Adolescence.* (London: Routledge, 1993).

2. Moore, S.M., Rosenthal, D.A. and Mitchell, A. (1996), *Youth, AIDS, and Sexually Transmitted Diseases* (London: Routledge, 1996).

3. Smith, E.A., Udry, J.R. and Morris, N.M. (1985), "Pubertal development and friends: A biosocial explanation of adolescent sexual behavior", *Journal of Health and Social Behavior*, 26: 183–92.

4. Rosenthal, D.A., Smith, A.M.A. and Reichler, H. "High schoolers' masturbatory practices: Their relationship to sexual intercourse and personal characteristics" *Psychological Reports*. (in press, 1997).

5. Rosenthal, D.A. and Smith, A.M.A. "Adolescent sexual timetables." *Journal of Adolescence* (in press, 1997).

6. Strubel, B. "The dating game: Young people talk about initiating romantic relationships." Paper presented at Second Annual Meeting of the Society of Australasian Social Psychologists (SASP), Canberra, April, 1996.

7. Moore, S.M. and Boldero, J. (1991), "Psychosocial development and friendship functions in young Australian adults." *Sex Roles*, 25: 521–36.

8. Erikson, E. *Identity, Youth and Crisis* (New York: Norton, 1968), 132.

9. Kinsey, A.C., Pomeroy, W.B. and Martin, C.E. *"Sexual Behavior in the Human Male"* (Philadelphia: Saunders, 1948).

10. Kinsey, A.C., Pomeroy, W.B., Martin, C.E. and Gebhard, P.H. *"Sexual Behavior in the Human Female"* (Philadelphia: Saunders, 1953).

11. Brooks-Gunn, J. and Furstenberg, F.F. Jr. (1989), "Adolescent sexual behavior" *American Psychologist* 44: 249–57.

12. Dusek, J.B. *Adolescent Development and Behavior* (New Jersey: Prentice-Hall, 1991)

13. Hofferth, S.L. and Hayes, C.D. (eds) *Risking the Future: Adolescent Sexuality, Pregnancy and Childbearing 1* (Washington D.C.: National Academy of Science, 1987).

14. Australian Institute of Family Studies, *Australian Family Formation Project, Study 1: A Longitudinal Survey of Australians aged 13 to 34 years* (Canberra: Australian National University Social Science Data Archives, 1981–2)

15. Goldman, R.J. and Goldman, J.D.G. *Show Me Yours: Understanding Children's Sexuality* (Ringwood: Penguin, 1988).

16. Johnson, A.M., Wadsworth, J., Wellings, K. and Field, J. *Sexual Attitudes and Lifestyles* (Oxford: Blackwell Scientific Publications, 1994).

17. Smith, A.M.A., de Visser, R., Akande, A., Rosenthal, D. A. and Moore, S.M. "Australian and South African university undergraduates' HIV-related knowledge, attitudes, and behaviours" *Archives of Sexual Behavior* (in press, 1997)

18. Thornton, A. and Camburn, D. (1987), "The influence of the family on premarital attitudes and behavior", *Demography*, 24: 323–40.

19. McCabe, M. and Collins, J. *Dating, Relating and Sex.* (Sydney: Horowitz Grahame, 1990)

20. Newcomer, S.J. and Udry, J.R. (1985), "Oral sex in an adolescent population" *Archives of Sexual Behavior* 14: 41–6.

21. Breakwell, G.M. and Fife-Schaw, C. (1992), "Sexual activities and preferences in a United Kingdom sample of 16–20 year olds" *Archives of Sexual Behaviour* 21: 271–93.

22. Dunne, M., Donald, M., Lucke, J., Nilsson, R. and Raphael, B. *National HIV/AIDS Evaluation 1992 HIV Risk and Sexual Behaviour Survey in Australian Secondary Schools: Final Report* (Canberra: Commonwealth Department of Health and Community Services, 1993).

23. Hingson, R. and Strunin, L. "Monitoring adolescents' responses to the AIDS epidemic: Changes in knowledge, attitudes, beliefs, and behaviours", in R.J. DiClemente (ed.) *Adolescents and Aids: A Generation in Jeopardy* (Newbury Park, CA: Sage, 1992).

24. Rosenthal, D.A. and Reichler, H. *Young Heterosexuals, HIV/AIDS, and STDs* (Canberra: Department of Human Services and Health, 1994).

25. Sorensen, R.E. *Adolescent Sexuality in Contemporary America*. (USA: World, 1973).

26. Rosenthal, D.A., Moore, S.M. and Brumen, I. (1990), "Ethnic group differences in adolescents' responses to AIDS" *Australian Journal of Social Issues* 25: 220–39.

27. Rosenthal, D.A., Moore, S.M. and Buzwell, S. (1994), "Homeless youths: Sexual and drug related behaviour, sexual beliefs and HIV/AIDS risk" *AIDS Care* 6: 83–94.

28. Buzwell, S., Rosenthal, D.A. and Moore, S.M. (1992), "Idealising the sexual experience" *Youth Studies Australia — HIV/AIDS Education* 1: 3–10.

29. Cochran, S.D. and Mays, V.M. (1990), "Sex, lies, and HIV [Letter

to the editor]" *New England Journal of Medicine* **322**: 774–5.

30. Smith, A.M.A. and Rosenthal, D. A. "Aspects of the social well-being of non heterosexual youth." Paper presented at First National Lesbian, Gay, Transgender and Bisexual Health Conference, Sydney, Australia, October, 1996.

31. Hillier, L., Warr, D. and Haste, B. *The Rural Mural: Sexuality and Diversity in Rural Youth*. (Research Report, Centre for the Study of Sexually Transmissible Diseases. Melbourne: La Trobe University, 1996).

FOUR

Sexual Relationships, Negotiation and Decision Making

Rachel Thomson and Janet Holland

Over the course of a generation there have been many changes in the attitudes and practices of adolescents, and this is nowhere so true as in the area of sexuality. Young people have become increasingly liberal and tolerant in the area of personal morality,[1] they are sexually active at an earlier age and there is growing evidence of convergence in the patterns of female and male sexual behaviour.[2] Yet there is also evidence of a 'gender lag' in these changes — the attitudes, expectations and aspirations of young women are changing more quickly than those of young men, and a significant proportion of young men continue to hold traditional expectations of gender roles.[3]

The religious and ethnic diversity of many developed societies means that there continues to be variation in attitudes towards sexual relationships and levels of sexual experience, but sexual activity is both statistically and culturally a 'normal' part of late adolescence. While it may be 'normal' for young people to have sex, evidence of regret and the inability of realising intentions to practice safer sex, suggest that many young people are uncertain about the pleasure, perils and precautions that are involved in sexual relationships.[4]

In this chapter we explore the social context of young people's sexual relationships, how expectations of conventional femininity and masculinity shape communication and decision making in their intimate encounters, and suggest practical ways in which those working with young people might address these issues. We draw on material from two studies undertaken by the authors[5] but the points that we raise in the chapter have been confirmed by many studies in Britain and other developed countries.[6]

Expectations and reality: First sex

The processes through which young people learn about sex are those through which they learn about being feminine and masculine, and young men and young women arrive at their first sexual experience with very different expectations.

How was it for him?

Becoming sexually active appears to be a crucial part of the process of moving from the status of a boy to that of a man:

"... I mean it's the old saying, 'you enter the bed a boy and you leave it a man' or words to that effect. I felt the same, I didn't alter physically, but I felt different after that first time. I did definitely feel different." (young man, aged 19, ESW[7], working class)

Studies with young men have found that sexual experience is highly prized within the male peer group and is generally understood as being inherently positive, even if it fails to meet with prior expectations. Young men experience pressure from their peers to be sexually active and knowledgeable, and sexual experience can provide them with a passport to status and affirmation. The opinions of male friends seemed to be paramount in the first sexual experiences of some of the young men in our study:

"At the time I was thinking, if only my mates could see me now, and stuff like that, and I must admit I didn't really think of the girl at the time." (young man, aged 16, African Caribbean, working class)

The dynamics of the adolescent male peer group mean that it can be difficult for young men to demonstrate ignorance or innocence about sex to their peers or to their sexual partners. They feel under pressure to 'do sex well' and often suffer anxiety about their 'performance'.

Q. "Did you feel confident?"

A. "No, I felt bloody nervous. I thought, what if I don't get a hard on? It all goes to pot." (young man, aged 19, ESW, working class)

This anxiety can eclipse concern for their partner and in our study was often associated with a preference for having first sexual encounters with partners whose judgements would not get back to their friends (for example holiday romances, older more experienced partners).

Q. "Is there a sort of feeling do you think amongst men to think they have to be good at sex?"

A. "I think so yes, especially if you have seen the girl about and stuff like that, and like you know she is going to open her mouth to everyone else if you are not good, so yes, you have to perform quite well, if you know the girl like, and you have seen her about." (young man, aged 16, African Caribbean, working class)

There were exceptions to this pattern, some young men had their first sexual experience in the context of longer term relationships and friendships, and in these cases there tended to be greater equality and communication:

Q. "How was it [with] both of you being virgins? Was it all right the first time? I mean sometimes it's a bit problematic."

A. "No, it was funny. I mean you've got to get rid of your embarrassment and you're both in the same boat. You both know, and it's just a laugh isn't it? It's not a ... I didn't find it like a nerve-racking experience like lot of people do. I just sort of took it as it comes. If it doesn't work the first time you have another go. You laugh about it." (young man, aged 18, white/Asian ethnicity; middle class)

How was it for her?

Although sexual practice has undergone enormous changes over a generation, sexual attitudes have not always kept pace. The convergence in the patterns of male and female sexual activity has not been entirely parallelled by a convergence in the social meanings associated with sexual behaviour. In many cultures conventional femininity continues to require that young women should not be seen to be sexually desiring or assertive, and while young men are expected to seek sexual access, young women are expected to resist their sexual advances. This can be illustrated by the words of the following young man interviewed in our study who questioned his partners claims to virginity on the basis of her unseemly lack of resistance to his advances.

Q. "Was it her first time?"

A. "She said it was but I — I don't know whether it was or not. Because like it was too quick like for her like, for a girl to say it was, like in a couple of hours. It would have been more if like she was a virgin, so I reckon she wasn't." (young man, aged 18, ESW, working class)

It appears that young men approach sex from the position of the sexual actor (the person who does sex) whereas young women are generally positioned as the objects of sex (the person who has sex done to them). The lack of power involved in the latter position (other than the negative power to 'say no') was apparent to many young women.

A. "And I suppose he must been on a right high, you know, just, you know, broke someone's virginity — a sixteen year old girl…" (young woman, aged 19, ESW, working class)

Many of the young women we interviewed found it difficult to articulate their own agency in such sexual encounters and frequently described sex as something that 'happened to them'. Faced only with the choice of saying no or yes to sex effectively silences any voice that a young woman may have in negotiating the context and meaning of the sexual encounter:

A. "… normally when you just know a boy's going to try it on or something, you know like, — and, you know, that's when you say 'No' or something, but I didn't. I wanted — I did want to do it. It wasn't like I was — like I say — I wasn't forced or anything. I knew what was going to happen and, you know, I wasn't worried." (young woman, aged 19, ESW, working class)

Young women in our study dealt with this lack of agency in different ways. Some sought to escape it by rushing into their first sexual experience and 'getting it over and done with'. Unfortunately this was frequently associated with frustration and regret:

Q. "Do you think you made the right decision the first time?"

A. "No. I suppose I wanted to just get it over and done with — I didn't want to rush into it, just because he was there, and I'd been going out with him anyway. I didn't like him. I just finished with him. I hated it. It's not great the first time. Never." (young woman, aged 18, ESW, working class)

A number of studies have documented the way in which being positioned as the objects of male sexual desire can render young women passive in heterosexual sexual relationships, irrespective of the existence of force or pressure on the part of male partners.[8] These studies have observed that being the object of male desire can effectively silence female desire and lead to self surveillance on the part of women both young and old. Self surveillance can be manifested as 'nurturance' (fulfilling the needs of their male partner) and/or pragmatism (accepting that consent to sexual experience may be easier than offering resistance). Many of the young women's accounts of their first sexual experiences reflect this ambivalence, and a frequent response to such confusion was self blame:

Q. "Why did you do it?"

A. "don't know. I liked him, but I don't know why — I wish i didn t do it." (young woman, aged 16, ESW, middle class)

The lack of emphasis on female sexual pleasure in formal and informal sex education and in the wider society, means that many young women enter sexual relationships aware of the sexual needs of men but without a clear sense of their own sexual self interest. As the following young woman explains:

A. "... if I could go back then and change my mind I would, not because I lost my virginity, but because he was so horrible [laughs]. But I can't. And it wasn't very nice, like it was —"

Q. "You didn't enjoy it?"

A. "Oh. Well, not like — you know, like you were saying do I like my job. But — because I've got nothing to compare it against, then you don't know. ... in one sense I think you might enjoy it because, you know, like you're having sex and, you know, you don't really know what to enjoy it is like." (young woman, aged 19, ESW, working class)

The contrasting accounts given by young men and young women of their first sexual experiences illustrate the differently gendered worlds within which adolescents become sexually active. Not all the young women in our study gave negative accounts of their first sexual experiences, but they reported significantly less satisfaction than did the young men.

The most positive accounts of first sexual experience tended to come from young people who were able to communicate openly with their partner and express their individual needs and desires within the privacy of a relationship or sexual encounter. It is important to remember that while adolescent sexual relationships may technically take place in private, they are located within complicated social networks of peers where information is exchanged and reputations are constructed. Conventional heterosexual identities are frequently enforced through the mechanism of sexual reputation, where a young woman is in danger of being labelled a 'slag' if she is seen to be sexually assertive and a young man is in danger of being labelled a 'wimp' or 'gay' if he is not.[9] The extent to which young people conform to or transgress conventional masculinity and femininity in their intimate relationships depends in part on the climate of the peer culture within which they are located.

Young people may also have a vested interest in not communicating about sex in early sexual encounters. One study found that silence can enable ambiguity to be maintained by both partners as to whether sex will actually happen. To mention condoms presumes that sex is on the cards, thereby opening the possibility of rejection. In the absence of communication the meanings and associations of conventional masculinity and femininity tend to fill the silence, overshadowing the needs and desires of the individuals involved and concerns for sexual safety. Commentators have observed that 'hegemonic masculinity' (a socially shared understanding of successful masculinity, constituted in opposition to femininity and other subordinate forms of masculinity including homosexuality) dominates the sexual cultures of both young and adult men and women.[10] Challenging hegemonic masculinity takes individual courage and may be punished by peers and partners. In the following section we explore the ways in which hegemonic masculinity and associated expectations frame the conditions within which sexual encounters are negotiated and which structure the possibilities of safer sex for young people.

Trusting to love: The logic of sexual risk taking

A number of studies have confirmed that unsafe sex, in terms of pregnancy and protection against sexually transmitted diseases is a 'normal' part of adolescent sexual experience. Unsafe sex is particularly associated with first sexual encounters, with those who begin their sexual career at a relatively early age and with those who have higher numbers of sexual partners.[11] In our studies we found that the practice of safer sex (particularly for protection against STDs) was uneven and inconsistent, and we have argued that this inconsistency is the outcome of the contradictory pressures of conventional masculinity and femininity on sexual encounters. The demands of conventional femininity militated directly against the demands of sexual health, and in many cases the former proved more compelling.

The belief that sexual decision-making is a rational, individual process predicated on free choice, has received sustained criticism, and it has been recognised that the arena of intimate sexual relations are subject to deeply rooted symbolic and social meanings and are structured by unequal power relationships.[12] If achieving safer sex was merely a process of rational decision making, the ability to negotiate would develop with growing experience and awareness. In contrast, we found that young people's ability to negotiate safer sex was conditional on the circumstances and contingencies of individual sexual encounters and relationships. Safer sex might be negotiated in one relationship but this did not necessarily imply that it could be successfully negotiated in the next. In some cases this negotiation was easier in early and 'casual' sexual encounters than in more established relationships, a finding that appears to hold for both heterosexual and gay relationships.[13]

The symbolic meanings of safer sex for heterosexuals also involves the meanings and practices associated with contraception. Developments in contraceptive technology have affected the meanings that we associate with heterosexual sex and the kind of sex that is practised. The move from the condom and withdrawal as the most common forms of contraception in the 1960's to the pill in the 1980's and 90's has been paralleled by a shift from men to women for the responsibility for sexual safety. The use of a particular contraceptive can profoundly construct both the expectation and practice of sex. The pill, unlike barrier methods, does not intrude on the act of sexual intercourse. Condoms are visible, require negotiation, disrupt the act of intercourse and bring attention to the potential for both pregnancy and disease. Within a culture where contraception has become an invisible female responsibility the negotiation of condom use can be highly disruptive.

Many of the young women to whom we spoke considered the 'spontaneity' enabled by the pill to be a central defining factor of sexual interaction and expressed opposition to condom use for reasons related to the disruption of this ideal. One young woman said:

"The climax to intercourse is all passion and kissing and I think to actually just stop and he puts a condom on, or me to turn around and say I want you to put this on, it just ruins the whole thing then"   (young woman, aged 20, ESW, middle class)

A young man specifically referred to the way in which condoms and the pill enable different kinds of sexual practice:

"Well condoms are a bit mechanical — not in themselves — it's just that you put one on, then you have sex under cover, then you take it off again. You can't sort of roll around with somebody for hours and sort of have penetrative sex, then stop that for a while, do something else, go back to that."   (young man, aged 20, ESW, middle class)

The belief that sex should be spontaneous is particularly attractive to young women, removing as it does the necessity of female sexual agency and masking a lack of confidence in and knowledge of their bodies. The 'rational' safer sex messages ('you know the risks, the choice is yours') can be seen as antithetical to discourses of conventional femininity, romance and passion which construct sex as relinquishing control in the face of love. Whether it is because it offers greater potential for pleasure and exploration, or because it requires less communication and engagement in the messy realities of sex, the understanding of sex made possible by the pill acts as a disincentive to the use of condoms and the practice of safer sex.

Symbolic meanings: Condoms, romance and trust

The dual imperatives on young people to protect against both pregnancy and sexually transmitted diseases complicates the practice of safer sex. Studies have found young people to be aware of the risks of HIV and AIDS (less so about other STDs) but more concerned about the possibility of pregnancy. Decision-making about the use of contraception and/or prophylactic protection in different sexual encounters ultimately owes as much to the symbolic meanings attached to these methods as to rational assessments of risk. Condoms are not neutral objects. They are associated with certain types of sex, significantly with sporadic sexual encounters, whether these are one night stands, early sexual experiences or sexual encounters outside an established relationship. Not using a condom is associated with the expression and demonstration of trust. The demonstration of trust is a significant factor in decision-making about condom use, and can in itself become a euphemism for monogamy or love.

In our studies we found that while condom use characterises the early stages of a sexual relationship, when a relationship was felt to be established, young people would often cease condom use and transfer to the pill as a method of contraception. Continued condom use at this point would distinguish between its function as prophylactic and contraceptive at a time when the display of trust is considered to be crucial. This transition from condoms with a new

partner to the pill with a steady partner is laden with symbolic meaning and can be used to signify the seriousness of a relationship, a
way of demonstrating to a partner that they are special. As one of
our respondents put it "I went on the pill for him". If condoms
signify 'casual', 'illicit' or inexperienced sex, the pill is associated
with grown up status and grown up sex. This makes the prospect of
long term condom use highly problematic, as some of our respondents clearly indicated:

"If you want to have relationships then you've got to trust them. Otherwise it's no good
from the start. You have to believe what they tell you. You just hope they tell the truth.
You can't find out if it's lies or not."   (young woman, aged 20, ESW, working class)

"You've got to trust somebody at some time, you can't meet somebody and start, first
time say, 'I know, let's use condoms I'm not on the pill" (even if you are) and then a week
later still be saying 'Let's use condoms' and a week after that still be saying 'Let's use
condoms'..."   (young woman, aged 21, ESW, working class)

But what is a 'serious', 'steady' or 'long term' relationship? We found
that there was a good deal of pressure on young women to define any
relationship they were in as 'serious' (and therefore steady) in order to
justify sex within a model of conventional femininity. Most young
women are reluctant to describe themselves as having casual sex when
the culturally approved objective is to be in a steady, preferably
monogamous relationship. They are likely to expect or to express the
hope that relationships of short duration, including one night stands,
will in fact last — relationships are 'steady' until proved otherwise.

A: "If I sleep with anyone I intend it to be a long term relationship — so I don't
know, because you don't like to think of the end of a relationship when you
start it."   (young woman, aged 16, ESW, working class)

In contrast, young men seemed much more able to see sexual
relationships as 'casual' and as potentially risky. The young men
in our study tended to distinguish sexual relationships with 'girlfriends' which were considered to be safe and sexual relationships
with 'slags' 'dodgy' and 'slack girls' which were considered to be
sexually risky.

"Safe sex is for a one-off. For one night stands it's alright, but for a long term relationships, I don't think — I think people who have long term relationships don't use condoms"   (young man, aged 18, white/Asian, middle class)

Power, pleasure and control in sexual situations

Perhaps the most important constraint experienced by young people wishing to practice safer heterosexual sex is the degree of control which they have within sexual encounters. In general we found that young women had far less control over their sexual encounters than did young men. One obvious way in which power is manifest in sexual relationships is the presence of violence or its threat. Pressure, ranging from rape to persuasion, was reported by a quarter of the young women in our study. Interviews with young men confirmed that 'persuasion' is a legitimate (even requisite) component of the masculine sexual role.

Yet power is present within sexual relationships in some far less explicit but still crucial ways. Research by ourselves and others has identified the privileging of male sexual pleasure as an important expression of power in sexual relationships that places young women at a significant disadvantage in negotiating safer sex.[14] One expression of the privileging of male sexual pleasure is the definition of what counts as sex. The majority of young men and women in our study understood sex to mean vaginal penetration (beginning with an erection and ending with ejaculation). Other sexual practices such as touching, mutual masturbation and oral sex were seen as either a prelude or afterthought to sexual intercourse. A significant proportion of the young women in the study reported that they experienced relatively little pleasure from sexual intercourse and relatively more from other forms of sexual practice but it was clear that vaginal intercourse was equated with 'real' and 'normal' sex.

Many of the young men's objections to condom use were centred on the way in which they disrupted their performance and pleasure.

"I think they're horrible, I never come with one"   (young man, aged 17, ESW, working class)

"They make your penis look pathetic"   (young man, aged 19, ESW, working class)

"It's like everything's ok, and then it's, Oh God, I've got to put a condom on' and then, you know, I kind of — I just lose my erection completely."   (young man, aged 17, ESW, working class)

Many of the objections to condom use, reported by young women in our study, were also related to ideas about male sexual pleasure and fears of its disruption. Both sexes used similar terms to describe the problems of condom use: 'having a bath with your boots on', 'eating a toffee with a wrapper on', but few cited criticisms which focussed on the ways in which condoms affect female pleasure. One young man reflected sensitively on this:

> Q: "Did she feel the same about it being sort of uncomfortable?"
>
> A: "It — well, yeah. I don't know. She said she didn't really like them. I don't know if it made an awful lot of difference to her really... But maybe she was also saying it because she knew I was uncomfortable about it."   (young man, aged 17, ESW, working class)

The privileging of male sexual pleasure within our culture is experienced particularly strongly by young women who are unsure of their own sexual potential and agency. The absence of sexual self interest on the part of young women involved in sexual relationships can place them at a disadvantage in the negotiation of sexual encounters. It is interesting that young women's reports of male opposition to condom use were not entirely confirmed by the reports of male respondents. This may be a characteristic of the sample (these were not the same young men with whom the young women were having sex) or may reflect the difficulties of communication between the sexes. It is possible that young women are policing their own behaviour, assuming male opposition to condoms, having internalised beliefs about the priority of male sexual pleasure. It was clear from our study that young women found consistent condom use very difficult. In our interview sample, 67 per cent of the sexually active young women had asked for condom use at some point in their sexual career. Of these 21 per cent had asked and had been refused for varying reasons. Others had not even been able to ask, finding themselves muted by the contradictions of their situation, and despite their intentions were unable to initiate condom use. In very few cases did young women report young men as taking responsibility in this area, and these were perceived to be exceptional.

A: "I know I have been in situations where I haven't [used a condom]. I have simply thought to myself, well look, well. When I got pregnant, I thought to myself, I'm not using a condom here, I'm not using anything, but I just couldn't say, just couldn't force myself to say, 'look you know' — and then the consequences were disastrous. But at the time I knew what I was doing, and I knew that I just couldn't say it and I knew that it was wrong."   (young woman, aged 21, ESW, working class)

A: "About two weeks ago I ended up not asking him [to use a condom] and had to go and get the morning after pill. I wouldn't say anything, and kept thinking I'll say something in a minute, it's just so difficult. I thought I'd say something in a minute and then it was too late, and I thought 'Oh no!' I didn't even know this person anyway."   (young woman, aged 18, ESW, middle class)

Strategies for safer sex

In this chapter we have shown that young women hold much of the responsibility for negotiating sexual safety, however the demands of conventional masculinity and femininity mean that they rarely have the power or the skills necessary to realise this responsibility. Yet young women are not simply passive victims and we found that many in our study were resourceful in their responses to this situation.

A small number of the young women we interviewed reported adopting a strategy of 'subterfuge', which entailed being on the pill but using its invisibility as a cover to request condom use on the basis of fear of pregnancy.

"Rather than saying, 'Will you wear something, because I don't want to get AIDS?' which sounds really bad, doesn't it, we would say, 'you'll have to wear something because I'm not on the pill' "   (young woman, aged 18, ESW, working class)

In this way, problems associated with trust, with appearances of sexual innocence and the taboo associated with the prophylactic function of the condom could effectively be avoided in the short term. The young women who used this strategy preferred it since it did not place them in the position of having to challenge the sexual politics of the sexual encounter. But it is also a strategy which demanded the acknowledgement of the transient nature of a sexual encounter, thereby challenging the romantic expectations of potential relationships. Not all young women are able to do this and the strategy became problematic if the relationship did in fact last.

A second strategy adopted by young women was the avoidance of vulnerability by establishing relationships with men who were younger and/or significantly less experienced or mature than themselves. This was usually not specifically in order to practice safer sex, but related to more general fears of vulnerability around sexuality and relationships. These young women seemed able to ensure that their own sexual needs were given status within their relationships. In most cases this included shared responsibility for sexual safety and contraception. A number of young men in our study also reported equivalent sexual relationships, characterised by openness, equality and mutual learning. Many of the young women involved in such relationships expressed concern that they might not be able to negotiate the same relationship with future partners, particularly if that partner was sexually experienced themselves.

Another group of young women who perceived themselves to be effectively 'safe' were those in monogamous relationships which they felt confident to actually be so. In a few cases the young women had negotiated an HIV test before the relationship became sexual. In others partners' sexual histories were known due to small and static social networks. The ability of young people to communicate openly and effectively about sexual histories has been shown to be problematic, while they may be able to communicate about numbers and names of sexual partners, it is more difficult to discuss details of sexual practice and condom use.[15] In effect it may be difficult to openly explore questions of 'risk' in the face of the imperatives of trust and commitment involved in negotiating a relationship, and partners remain vulnerable to the possibility of infidelity. The safety of such relationships were often based on informal judgements as to the moral categories into which partners were seen to fall. For many young men, these categories divided into 'girlfriends' and 'slags', while contraception would be used with the former, prophylactic protection might be used with the latter. For young women such distinctions were harder to make.

A small number of the young women to whom we spoke had considered safer sex to be a more significant project going far beyond condom use and part of a wider reconsideration of their own sexual practice, pleasure and desire. They were young women who had reflected upon their sexual experiences and found them wanting in terms of their own agency and access to sexual pleasure. The safer sex repertoire of these young heterosexual women was considerably wider than those who perceived it simply to mean using a condom and they were prepared to have to educate their partners about the validity and worth of a range of non-penetrative sexual practices. These young women experienced few if any problems negotiating condom use within this context. Such a strategy was effective precisely because it entailed challenging a definition of sex structured by expectations of men's needs and desires and in doing so the implicit constraints to safer sex as mentioned above, spontaneity, loss of control, trusting to love and lack of self esteem. Unlike the others described above, this particular strategy was not dependent on the context of the sexual encounter or relationship but could travel with the person from relationship to relationship.

One young woman described her understanding of safer sex and the means by which she employed these practices as follows:

> A: "Safe sex is as pleasurable an experience as actual penetration. Oral sex, just things like touching somebody else's body in a very gentle way. Kissing. Appreciating one another's bodies.

"I think it's just as [much] fun, if not more. You concentrate on each others needs a lot more, you're a lot more aware of them. You're aware of each others bodies a lot more.. Instead of 20 minutes of bang, bang bang, you've got a whole night; you watch the dawn come up and you're still there."

Q: "Have you had to convert your partners? Have you come across men who understand sex as being more than penetration?"

A: "Yes...I've said, 'I don't want to do that', or 'why don't you try this?'. Before they know it they're converted, and they suddenly realise — 'well we haven't actually done it'. — 'Well I'm tired now, haven't you had a good time?' You can change a lot of people's ideas."   (young woman, aged 18, ESW, working class)

It takes a special combination of circumstance and communication for young women to gain sufficient control in sexual encounters to ensure sexual safety, a secure feminine identity and their own sexual pleasure. Maintaining a sense of personal empowerment which is independent of context and relationship can be difficult and lonely. It requires young women to negotiate a new model of sexuality which treats female sexual pleasure as a priority. While the accounts that we received from young men in our study suggest that some felt threatened by sexually knowing and confident young women, there also existed a minority who welcome this change.

Masculinity and femininity are mutually dependent. Effecting change in one leads to changes in the other. The development of a positive sexual agency for young women will mean that young men must also be prepared to re-evaluate their own beliefs about masculine sexuality. The evidence from studies with young people suggests that the individual needs and desires of young men and women, both heterosexual and gay, are constrained by conventional masculinity and femininity and that they all share a vested interest in such changes.

Implications for practice and conclusions

Many of the issues that we have identified in this chapter can only be approached through education. Currently sex education tends to focus on girls, on the dangers of pregnancy and the facts of reproduction. Young men appear to receive substantially less education from all sources. The sex education that young people do receive does little to challenge the definitions of conventional masculinity and femininity which dominate and constrain adolescent sexual culture. It is important that sex education addresses the real needs and experiences of both sexes and concentrates on the meanings that young people associate with sexuality and the skills necessary to put their intentions into practice.

There is an urgent need for sex education to nurture and develop in young women a sense of self worth and self esteem and ally this to an awareness of their own sexual needs, desires and capacities, including that of sexual pleasure. Research with young men and women suggests that both are aware of women's reproductive capacities yet largely unaware of the potential for female sexual pleasure. Sex tends to be understood as something that a man does to a woman, and which a woman can give a man. Sex education programmes also need to encourage communication between the sexes. As we have suggested, conventional notions of masculinity and femininity are only able to dominate in silence, and research in this area suggests a high degree of misunderstanding and lack of effective communication between young people in sexual encounters. Sex education can clarify these assumptions and misunderstandings, enable open communication in safe environments and help to redress the balance of responsibility for sexual health.

Sex education also needs to address the impact of the peer group, in particular its role in the construction and policing of sexual reputations. Young men in particular experience considerable pressure from their peer group to become sexually active and to adopt an instrumental approach towards sexual relationships. There is a clear need for young men's fears of failure and vulnerability in relation to sexual performance to be recognised and licensed in sex education. The processes through which male peer groups dominate the language and meaning of the sexual has a negative impact on both young men and women and on their ability to communicate openly with each other. There continues to be great potential for informal approaches to sex education, both in terms of the development of community based peer education strategies and attempts to influence young people's sexual cultures through the media to which they have access. There are relatively few role models for young people in this area, and if we wish them to challenge conventional notions of masculinity and femininity we need to provide positive and accessible examples of such identities, and to reward attempts to develop other ways of being. The institutions within which young people spend much of their lives often act to reinforce traditional gender roles and either punish, or are complicit in the punishment of their transgression.

If services and education in sexual health are to be effective they need to incorporate an awareness of the way in which contraceptive choices can influence and structure sexual interaction, reinforcing the centrality of spontaneity and related ideas of loss of control as defining features of sex. The difficulties young women may have in defining sexual encounters as other than steady, despite objective circumstances, highlights a need to be sensitive to the use of language in sexual health counselling and education. Education and services directed at young people must also recognise the problems of consistent long term condom use within 'steady relationships' and the symbolic meanings attributed to condoms. Inevitably this requires the recognition within sexual health education of the limitations of condom use and a willingness to discuss and explain the possibilities of non-penetrative sex to young people in a way which is sensitive to their level of sexual experience.

Safer sex strategies which focus exclusively on the use of condoms will have limited effect and fail to provide a positive long term strategy for young people which challenges the disempowering norms of our sexual culture. Safer sex strategies need to be grounded in a knowledge of both female and male sexuality. The focus on condom use compounds the invisibility of female sexuality in our culture. The lesson from the gay community has been that people must feel some ownership of their sexuality before they feel able to control, shape and change their sexual practice. An emphasis on what we might call the 'possibilities of non-penetrative sex' is primarily a means by which to encourage young people both individually and collectively to challenge the norms of heterosexual sexual culture rather than a strict alternative to the use of condoms. This is a project with relevance not only for the fight against HIV/ AIDS but also for wider issues of effective contraception, informed decision making and sexual health in the broadest sense.

References

1. Halpern, D. (1995), 'Values, morals and modernity: the values, constraints and norms of European youth' in Rutter, M. and Smith, D. *Psychosocial disorders in young people: Time trends and their causes*, Chichester: Academia Europa.

2. Wellings, K., Field, J., Johnson, A.M. and Wadsworth, J. (1994), *Sexual behaviour in Britain*, London: Penguin.

3. Oakley, A. (1996), 'Gender matters: Man the hunter' in Roberts, H. and Sachdev, D. (Eds.) *Young people's social attitudes — having their say: The views of 12–19 year olds*, London: Barnardo's; Wilkinson, H. (1994) *No turning back: Generations and the genderquake*, London: Demos.

4. Wellings, K. *et al.* (1994), *op. cit.*

5. The Women, Risk and AIDS Project (1988–1990), staffed by the authors, Caroline Ramazanoglu, Sue Sharpe and Sue Scott. The Men Risk and AIDS Project (1991–1992) staffed by the authors, Caroline Ramazanoglu, Sue Sharpe and Tim Rhodes.

6. See: Wight, D. (1992), 'Impediments to safer heterosexual sex: A review of research with young people', *AIDS Care*, 4(1): 11–12; Kippax, S., Crawford, J. Waldby, C. and Benton, P. (1990) 'Women negotiating heterosex: Implications for AIDS prevention' *Women's Studies International Forum* 13: 533–42; Moore, S. M. and Rosenthal, D. A. (1992) 'The social context of adolescent sexuality: Safe sex implications', *Journal of Adolescence*, 6: 164–180; Reinders, J. and Vermeer, V. (Eds.) (1995) *Gender specific AIDS prevention for youth: A working document*, Utrecht: Dutch Centre for Health Promotion and Health Education.

7. 'ESW' indicates 'English/Scottish/Welsh' which was used in our purposive sample as a category of ethnic origin.

8. See: Gavey, N. (1992), 'Technologies and effects or heterosexual coercion' in Kitzinger, C., Wilkinson, S. and Perkins, R. (Eds.) *Special issue on heterosexuality: Feminism and Psychology* 2(3):774–5; Kippax, S., *et al.* (1990) *op. cit.*; Donovan, C. (1996) 'Young people, alcohol and sex: Taking advantage' *Youth and Policy*, 52:30–37; Fine, M. (1988) 'Sexuality, schooling and adolescent females: The missing discourse of desire' *Harvard Educational Review*, 58(1): 29–53.

9. See: Lees, S. (1993), *Sugar and spice: Sexuality and adolescent girls*, London: Penguin; Holland, J., Ramazanoglu, C., Sharpe, S. and Thomson, R. (1996) 'Reputations: Journeying into gendered power relations' in Weeks, J. and

Holland, J. (Eds.) *Sexual cultures: Communities, values and intimacy*, London: Macmillan.

10. Connell, R.W. (1995), *Masculinities*, Cambridge: Polity Press.

11. Wellings, K. *et al.* (1994), *op. cit.*

12. Wight, D. (1992), *op. cit.*

13. Weatherburn, P. *et al.* (1992), *The sexual lifestyles of gay and bisexual men in England and Wales*, London: Project Sigma; Frankham, J. (1996) *Young gay men and HIV infection*, London: AVERT.

14. Holland, J., Ramazanoglu, C., Scott, S., Sharpe, S. and Thomson, R. (1990), *'Don't die of ignorance' I nearly died of embarrassment: Condoms in context*, London: The Tufnell Press; Holland, J., Ramazanoglu, C., and Sharpe, S. (1993), *Wimp or gladiator: Contradictions in acquiring masculine sexuality*, London: The Tufnell Press; Gavey, N. (1992), *op. cit.*; Kippax *et al.* (1990), *op. cit.*; Richardson, D. (1996), 'Contradictions in discourse: Gender, sexuality and HIV/AIDS' in Holland, J. and Adkins, L. (Eds.) *Sex, sensibility and the gendered body*, London: Macmillan.

15. Ingham, R., Woodcock, A. and Stenner, K. (1991), 'Getting to know you... young people's knowledge of their partners at first intercourse' *Journal of Community and Applied Psychology*, 1: 117–132.

FIVE

Risks Associated with Early Sexual Activity and Fertility

Kaye Wellings and Kirsti Mitchell

Introduction

Recent decades have witnessed substantial change in the sexual behaviour and attitudes of young people. Sex currently assumes a greater significance in the lives of young people than was formerly the case. High levels of sexual activity at an early age puts young people at greater risk of outcomes such as teenage pregnancy which adversely affect future life chances.

This chapter explores the risk factors associated with teenage sexual activity. It begins by looking at the risk factors associated with two aspects of sexual behaviour which have an impact on the likelihood of teenage pregnancy; age at first intercourse and contraceptive use. The social and biological consequences of teenage pregnancy are then examined and the implications for policy are discussed.

The data comes predominantly from the National Survey of Sexual Attitudes and Lifestyles (NSSAL) carried out in 1990 and 1991[1] since this survey presents the most up-to-date and comprehensive picture of British sexual behaviour (Note 1). The survey is based on a sample of 18, 876 respondents aged 16 to 59, randomly selected from the Post Office small-users Postcode Address File (PAF). Respondents underwent personal interviews combining both face-to-face and self-completion components. The interview began with questions about general health, family circumstances, memories of sex education and early sexual experiences. It moved on to ask about sexual orientation, numbers of partners and frequency and nature of different sexual practices.

Factors associated with early intercourse

Recent trends in age at first intercourse

During the last 30 to 40 years there has been a dramatic fall in the age at which young people become sexually active. Over the past four decades, the median age at first intercourse (the age by which half of young people have experienced first intercourse) has fallen from 21 to 17 for women, and from 20 to 17 for men. Moreover this trend has been coupled with an increase in the number of young people who have sexual intercourse before the legal age of consent (Note 2). At present nearly one in five women and more than one in four men under the age of 20 have had intercourse before this age. Furthermore, young women particularly tend to be in a greater hurry to develop their sexual experience, (Note 3) progressing from first sexual encounter to first intercourse in only years. Young men, on the other hand, take three years to make this step.

These trends suggest that traditional gender differences in early sexual experience are becoming less marked. Yet despite the convergence in behaviour, young women are more prone to regret early intercourse. In fact, more than a third of women aged 16 to 24 considered their first experience of intercourse to have been too soon. This figure rises to 50% for those who were under 16 at the time. The fact that young men are far less likely to express regret perhaps reflects different expectations of first intercourse. While young men are most commonly driven by curiosity, young women are more likely to say they engaged in first intercourse because they were in love. This may explain why many young women are often disappointed by their first experience of intercourse. Cultural influences such as the media may add to the disappointment by raising expectations beyond the realms of reality.

Early experience of sexual intercourse is also associated with higher numbers of sexual partners subsequently, and is less likely to be protected from unplanned pregnancy. It is therefore important to work towards an understanding of the demographic and situational risk factors associated with early first intercourse.

Socio-demographic risk factors

Striking social class differences in age at first intercourse were found in the 1950s[2, 3] with working class adolescents experiencing sexual intercourse at an earlier age than those from the middle classes. These differences appear to have persisted in the UK and, to a lesser extent, throughout Europe and the US. Young people (aged 16–24) in social classes I and II currently experience first sexual intercourse at 18, a full two years after those in classes IV and V.

Level of educational attainment also has a significant effect on the age at first intercourse, with those undertaking higher education delaying first intercourse until 18, one year later than school leavers with qualifications. Those who leave school with no qualifications at all experience first intercourse earliest, at 16. Those who undertake further education are particularly unlikely to experience early sex. Compared with their non-graduate peers, graduate men are more than four times less likely to have had sex before their sixteenth birthday, and non-graduate women less than twice as likely. The mechanisms by which social class and education impact on teenage sexual behaviour are explored later in the chapter.

Age at first sexual intercourse varies significantly by ethnic origin. Cultural beliefs and attitudes particular to each ethnic group are likely to play a part, as well as structural factors such as family income which vary by ethnic group and have an influence on early sexual behaviour. Young people of Bangladeshi and Indian origin are much less likely to report sexual intercourse having occurred before the age of 16 (10.7% of men and 1.1% of women compared with 18.8% of men and 7.0% of women from all ethnic groups combined). Interestingly, gender differences in age at first intercourse are more pronounced within minority ethnic groups, perhaps reflecting greater demarcation of gender roles.

Adherence to a religious group appears to protect against early intercourse. Roughly 23% of men and 12% of women who claim no religious affiliation experience intercourse before the age of 16, compared with 19% of men and 9% of women belonging to any religious group. Belonging to a religion may have a direct impact on sexual behaviour through adherence to specific moral codes. However, it may be that the effects of religious beliefs and sexual behaviour are reciprocal. Sexual behaviour may reflect the influence of religious values on a young person, but conversely, religious beliefs which do not support the pattern of behaviour preferred by an adolescent may be allowed to lapse. Furthermore, where religious affiliation arises from socio-cultural factors such as family background, ethnicity and area of residence, it may also have a more diffuse effect on behaviour.

Situational risk factors

Social pressure, particularly from peers, is often cited as a reason for young people having intercourse for the first time. The 'herding instinct' is thought to be particularly exaggerated in the teenage years when conformity to a group norm and identity is particularly important. Previous studies of sexual behaviour were equivocal about the influence of group membership but identified a widespread belief among teenagers that others of their age are more sexually active than themselves. [4] The NSSAL study suggests that group norms are not a key factor for either sex but may contribute towards the decision to have sex. Young men are more susceptible to this peer influence than young women — 8% of men and 4% of women claimed that the main reason they first had sexual intercourse was that most friends their age seemed to be doing it. Since it is important to many young people to view their first experience of intercourse as a personal choice, then it is worth considering that they may be reluctant to admit peer influence as a contributing factor. Furthermore peer influence tends to be subtle and indirect, such that some young people may not be aware of its existence at the time. The pressure on young men to lose their virginity appears to be increasing. Of young men aged 16–24, 11% gave this as the most important factor associated with first intercourse compared with only 2% of men aged 45 to 59. In contrast, contemporary young women are rarely likely to cite this as a factor.

Alcohol is often used as a scapegoat to explain (or excuse) early or unwanted sex. Although alcohol has often been consumed at the time of first intercourse, there is little evidence of it being a major precipitating factor. Although the association between first intercourse and drinking has increased in younger generations, only 5% of women and 6% of men in the 16 to 24 year age group report being slightly drunk as the main factor associated with their loss of virginity, while 14% of men and 10% of women cite it as a contributory factor. Alcohol is more likely to be mentioned by those for whom intercourse occurred at an early age.

Interestingly, the whole experience of first intercourse seems to have been the subject of more planning and less spontaneity in recent decades. Reporting method used in the previous year, younger women are less likely than older women to report first intercourse occurring because they were 'carried away by their feelings'. This is consistent with the findings of recent US studies. More than half of teenagers in one such study said they had discussed their first sexual experience with their prospective partner prior to having sex, although this was true more often for females than males.[5]

Contraceptive use by young people

Trends in contraceptive use

Despite an earlier start to sexual activity, young people today seem to be more efficient contraceptors than were those in previous generations. The number of teenagers using contraception in recent times has increased, although not always consistently.[6] According to the NSSAL survey, the proportion of young women whose experience of first intercourse was not protected has declined steadily over the past four decades. Condoms are easily the most popular method of contraception for first sexual intercourse. Half of young women report using a condom on their first occasion of sex compared with 20% reporting the pill and 24% reporting no method at all.

Equally important is the pattern of on-going contraceptive practice. Reporting method used in the previous year, young men most frequently cite the condom (60.8%), followed by the pill (53.1%). Young women reported using the pill most frequently (64.1%), followed closely by the condom (41.9%). (Note 4) Around 9% of young people use no contraception on a regular basis. The NSSAL survey measured the prevalence of unsafe sex, broadly defining it as 'having 2 or more heterosexual partners in the last year but never using a condom in that time'. Using this definition 9.7% of men and 9.2% of women (aged 16–24) currently practice unsafe sex. These percentages are likely to be underestimates however, since those using condoms inconsistently and those at risk as a result of their partner's behaviour are excluded.

Risk factors for unprotected intercourse

Age at first intercourse is an important risk factor for unprotected sex. The younger the person at the time of first intercourse, the greater the likelihood that first intercourse will be unprotected. Nearly half of young women and more than half of young men who have intercourse before the age of 16 report no method used either by themselves or by a partner. This proportion falls sharply to 32% of women and 36% of men aged 16 and over at first intercourse.

There are several reasons for failure to protect early intercourse. Young people may be reluctant to seek contraceptive supplies or advice for an act which, if it involves a young woman under the age of 16, is against the law. Legal issues notwithstanding, purchasing condoms is widely regarded as an embarrassing activity, and many young people are anxious about being caught in possession of condoms either by friends or parents. Those who carry condoms may earn a reputation of promiscuity, since carrying condoms suggests that sex has been planned in advance. Young women particularly, run the risk of being labelled as a 'slag'. Research suggests that even if condoms are carried, factors such as drunkenness, 'losing control and not caring' and worry about partner reaction to the idea of condoms means that they will not necessarily be used. In addition, lack of self-esteem and confidence may deter young people both from acquiring contraception and from raising the issue with partners.

Power imbalances typical of young heterosexual relationships mean that lack of self esteem and confidence are particularly salient issues for young women. Perhaps more than males, they lack a suitable script with which to negotiate safe sex. Interviews with young women suggest that whilst some are confident enough to insist on condoms being used others, especially younger women, are less sure of themselves and struggle to know what to say if the man offers any resistance to a suggestion that he should wear a condom. Young women whose primary experience of sexual relations has been one of male dominance may already anticipate that the man will get his way and may therefore be less inclined to pursue their own interests in negotiating contraceptive use.[7]

The less well two young people know each other the more likely they are to have unprotected intercourse. In the NSSAL survey more than two thirds of women whose partner at first intercourse was someone they had met for the first time used no contraception, compared with fewer than half of those for whom it was someone they had met recently, and fewer than a third in a steady relationship. Early sexual experience is significantly associated with short-term relationships and failure to protect intercourse might therefore reflect the sporadic nature of sexual activity at this age.

Teenagers may delay seeking contraceptive advice until a relationship has become established.[8] Some young people find it difficult to accept that they need contraception at all, since they may not intend to have intercourse until it actually occurs. Although planned intercourse is more common among young people today than in previous generations, there remains more than a quarter of young people who have first intercourse on the 'spur of the moment'. Not surprisingly, first sexual intercourse occurring spontaneously is far less likely to be protected. Young people also tend to make unrealistic assessments of the risks of becoming pregnant, believing that 'it will never happen to them'. [9]

Factors associated with teenage pregnancy

Trends in teenage pregnancy

Data from the Office of National Statistics (ONS) shows that 29% of women in the UK conceive between the ages of 15 and 19, and just over half of these conceptions end in a live birth. There are no equivalent figures for men but only 4% of men in the NSSAL survey report having fathered a child before the age of 20. The gender difference may be partly explained by the age difference of around two years in partnerships between men and women so that many of the fathers of children born to women in their teens would be 20 or older. But there is also a strong possibility that many men father a child unwittingly.

The teenage birth rate rose in the late 1950s and accelerated in the 1960s to peak at around 1970, when 17% of women and 6% of men had a child in their teens. During the late seventies and early eighties considerable success was achieved in reducing the teenage pregnancy rate though some of these gains have been lost more recently. Living in the British isles itself seems to be a strong risk factor for teenage motherhood. England has the worst teenage pregnancy rates in Europe, followed closely by Scotland and N. Ireland.

Risk factors associated with teenage pregnancy

Patterns of risk seem to be established early in the teenage years. Not surprisingly, the earlier young men and women begin sexual activity, the higher the chance that they will have a child in their teens: those who have sexual intercourse before the age of 16 are four times more likely to become parents before 20 than those who delay sexual activity. Failure to use a contraceptive method at first intercourse is also strongly associated with teenage birth.

Ignorance about sexual matters is a crucial risk factor and seems to have a stronger influence on whether teenage sexual activity results in birth than it has on the timing of its first occurrence. Lack of planning at first intercourse is also linked with teenage birth; teenage motherhood is more common amongst those for whom the event was spontaneous than among those who thought ahead. In general, older teenagers are better informed about birth control and more likely to plan intercourse. This may be attributable to developmental factors and to cognitive and psychological maturity.

Family influences

The sexual activity and parenthood patterns of teenagers are strongly associated with characteristics of the family in which they grow up. Women from larger than average families, who live with only one parent as a child, and who have parents who have been divorced, separated or bereaved are more likely than other groups of women to give birth early. [10] Studies have shown adolescents — daughters in particular — from single parent families begin sexual intercourse earlier and are more likely to be parents themselves early in life. [11]

Teenage sexual activity and parenthood are also strongly influenced by the environment of the family — by the ease and extent of discussion about sex, by parental attitudes towards teenage sexuality and by the degree of discipline and constraint exerted over young people in the family. Many of the factors related to family structure and environment are clearly linked in their effects. Research suggests that there may be less parental supervision in single parent households both because there is one less parent and because single mothers are more likely to work full time than are mothers in two parent households. The number of children in the family can be expected to significantly determine both level of discipline and extent of communication. And whether there is one parent or two will help determine the pattern of role modelling, as for example where single parents are themselves in sexual relationships. Single or separated parents have been found more likely to discuss sex, pregnancy and birth control than parents in intact marriages.[12]

Of all these factors, the one which seems to have the strongest protective effect on teenage pregnancy is discussion about sex. Studies have found greater communication within the family to be associated with a lower probability of early sexual activity and an increased likelihood of use of birth control.[10]

Women who have a baby early in life are more likely to come from larger families themselves and are more likely to go on to have more children subsequently. At the same time women with larger numbers of siblings who do not have a baby early in life are also more likely to have larger numbers of children. The key question is then whether family patterns are simply repeated through subsequent generations. But irrespective of the size of the family young people grow up in, those who have a child early in life are more likely to have larger numbers of children than those who delay childbearing. Data from NSSAL shows that respondents who were parents in their teens had more children regardless of the size of the family they themselves were born into.[10]

Educational chances

Women with no educational qualifications are very much more likely to have a child before 20 than those with some, and likelihood decreases progressively with level of educational attainment. Teenage birth is rare among graduate women. Likelihood of abortion is also linked with educational level, though less strongly, and the effect is reversed, i.e. the higher the educational level the more likely a young woman is to terminate a pregnancy.

The earlier in a woman's teens the first birth occurs, the poorer are her educational prospects. The low level of educational attainment amongst women who enter motherhood at an early age is an important factor determining life chances, since lack of qualifications will compound the barriers to employment resulting from difficulties of child care and of balancing responsibilities of early motherhood and work.

Early sexual experience and educational attainment each have an independent effect on teenage pregnancy, and so combine to increase the risk. Those for whom educational prospects are poor are more likely to become sexually active, more likely to conceive if they are sexually active, and more likely to have a live birth if they conceive.[10]

Of interest here is the extent to which lack of progress in school might itself lead to early parenthood versus the extent to which early parenthood damages educational prospects. It has been suggested that early sexual experience serves to enhance self esteem which might otherwise be sought in educational achievement, and that some sense of purpose and individual fulfilment may be found in teenage motherhood which seems unattainable academically. Those for whom academic aspirations seem remote may be more likely to seek achievement and satisfaction in early relationships, and subsequently in early motherhood, than those for whom educational goals are more of an attainable reality. At the same time those who become pregnant in their teens are likely to experience considerable disruption of their studies as a result of pregnancy and child rearing.

Table 1 Prevalence of abortion and teen birth by education: women aged 20–24

	Degree	Higher/ A level	O-level/ CSE	None
		All women aged 20–24		
	%	%	%	%
Teen birth + abortion by age 24	0.0	0.6	1.9	10.4
Teen birth only	0.0	2.4	16.2	31.8
Abortion by age 24 only	15.8	10.7	11.1	5.8
No teen birth or abortion	84.2	86.3	70.8	52.0
Base	90	403	541	157

Health risks of teenage fertility

Biologically, pregnancy in the early years of reproductive life is not in itself harmful, and well managed pregnancies carry no higher risk in this age group, but in practice they are associated with a higher incidence of negative outcomes. Complications during teenage pregnancy include higher risks of anaemia, toxaemia, and hyper-tension; low birth weight babies, higher risks of perinatal mortality of infants; and a higher incidence of spontaneous abortions in subsequent pregnancies. Other studies, however, which control for possible confounding variables such as socio-economic status, nutrition, race, prenatal care etc. reveal fewer differences in obstetric and paediatric outcome with maternal age. [13]

Men, and more particularly women, who become parents early in life are more likely to report poor health status in their later lives, than those who do not. They are also more likely to be smokers. Women who had their first child in their teens are nearly twice as likely to be cigarette smokers and this effect is sustained after controlling for current age, educational level, age at first intercourse, social class and alcohol consumption. [10] Health status differences persist after controlling for current smoking behaviour, and so poorer health cannot be attributed solely to smoking cigarettes. Nor can it be attributed to alcohol consumption since teenage mothers are not significantly heavier drinkers than those who delay motherhood.

No consistent 'risk profile' in terms of the existence of a syndrome of risky practices has been identified. Some research suggests that smoking, alcohol and drug use, and early onset of sexual intercourse tend to occur among the same teenagers and may constitute a syndrome of risk taking behaviour. The explanation for this may be situational; these activities take place in similar settings, (i.e. young people in search of sexual encounters are likely to frequent those venues in which drinking and smoking takes place), or behavioural (i.e. some individuals may exhibit a consistent profile across different risk activities; those predisposed to drink heavily might also

smoke and take risks in terms of their sexual and reproductive behaviour) — a 'sensation-seeking' personality.

Early pregnancy does not seem to be part of a syndrome of risk-
taking tendencies which includes both smoking and drinking. The
explanation for the relationship between smoking and teenage
motherhood is probably better understood in terms of a general
lifestyle theory. Qualitative work in this area has demonstrated clearly
the role of stress in motivating smoking habits. Graham's study of
smoking among mothers, for example, has shown that for young
women with large families and little support, who live in straitened
circumstances, smoking might be one of the few pleasurable activities
in life with which to alleviate stress, and is viewed as such by the
women themselves.[14] The association might also be explained in
terms of situational factors. Women at home with children may
have more opportunities for smoking than drinking.

Social risks of teenage fertility — the effect on life chances

Generally it is the social rather than the physical or health related
consequences of early parenthood which are highlighted as
problematic. There is evidence that women who have early pregnancies complete their education early, have poorer employment prospects and are more likely to become dependent on welfare subsidies.[11]
They tend to leave home earlier and are more likely to live currently
in subsidised housing. Both teenage mothers and fathers are more
likely to be currently unemployed and mothers are more likely to be
looking after the home. Women who have a child early are also more
likely to be divorced later in life than those who do not.

There is evidence too, to suggest that children born to teenage
mothers may also be disadvantaged; research shows them to be
more vulnerable to accidental and non-accidental injuries, to be at
greater risk of physical abuse, to have lower scores on developmental
tests and to perform less well educationally than children of older
mothers.

These findings have not gone unquestioned. Studies controlling for parity (i.e. numbers of children born) show differences between older and younger mothers are greatly reduced. Others have found that controlling for various factors correlated with social class considerably weakens the effect of other variables.[15] Many of the adverse outcomes seem more likely to be results of poor socio-economic circumstances of women who give birth before 20.

Little attention is paid to how these outcomes are viewed by those individuals involved. Outcomes which are generally accepted as being undesirable — poor prospects relating to educational attainment, employment status or home ownership — may not be accepted as such by those directly affected and may be offset by the perceived advantages of having a child early in life. The birth of a child may be the one thing that redeems an otherwise impoverished life. The costs of teenage birth then may be compensated for by benefits of which not enough is known. Whether early fertility is *seen* as regrettable, or is in reality regretted by young parents, is largely an empirical question best answered by the mothers and fathers themselves.

Early parenthood is more common in mining, industrial areas and urban areas than it is in more prosperous, growing or rural areas. When the effects of parity, area of residence and social class on teenage motherhood are examined together, there is no greater likelihood of a woman who had a child early in life being in a manual social class. Area of residence remains a significant factor however, strongly suggesting the existence of an 'area' effect.

Deprived areas are characterised by higher rates of teenage pregnancy. One study found pregnancy rates in under 16 year olds to be three times as high, and in those under the age of twenty, six times as high, in the most deprived areas compared with the most affluent areas. Another study showed district health authorities with high underprivileged area scores (UPAs) to be more likely to have high rates of teenage conceptions than in those districts with low scores while a third discovered that Northern regions had more teenage conceptions and fewer abortions.

There is little evidence to suggest that more affluent areas are better served by birth control and young people's services. Factors linked with social disadvantage and local culture probably have more impact on teenage pregnancy than mere availability of health and family planning services.

Pathways of deprivation

It has been suggested that the material circumstances of young women and their partners would not necessarily improve if they deferred parenthood. Some have questioned the assumption that motherhood is riskier for younger women arguing that it is a more likely consequence of the cluster of factors which affect all those in deprived circumstances. A study of 16–25 year olds showed no difference between 16–19 year olds and 20–25 year olds in terms of social support, material circumstances and life chances.[16] A high proportion left school at the minimum leaving age, lacked qualifications and were unemployed but these problems, although associated with pregnancy, preceded it. This effect may operate through a perceived lack of options for the future. The view of these observers is that it may not be early motherhood *per se* which is problematic but the pre-existing socio-economic circumstances.

Whatever the extent to which teenage birth results from hardship and deprivation, it is clear that it also contributes to the risk of such outcomes. After taking into account the effects of education and social class, women who give birth in their teens are more likely to live in a poor area of the country, are less likely to own their home, and are less likely to be in paid work, than are those who did not. All other things considered, if young women and their partners defer parenthood, they will have greater opportunities for training, jobs and financial betterment.

Conclusion — implications for policy

Although there is a strong possibility that the birth of a child may be seen as compensation for some of life's disadvantages there are clearly adverse consequences for young mothers having a baby early in life. The aims of policy intervention should be twofold; firstly, the prevention of teenage births which are unplanned and unintended, and secondly, a reduction in the adverse consequences arising from births occurring at an early age but which are planned and intended.

It is often assumed that the constellation of factors associated with early motherhood are so inextricably linked as to be not amenable to manipulation. However, the strong association between age at first intercourse, contraceptive use at first intercourse, educational level and likelihood of teenage birth, and the fact that each of these associations remains independent after taking into account the effect of the others, implies that intervention focusing on any of these events has the potential to be effective in reducing the teenage birth rate.

Increasing knowledge

Receipt of adequate information is strongly linked with avoidance of teenage pregnancy and highlights the need to provide adequate sex education in this area. The strong association between ignorance about sexual matters and likelihood of teenage birth implies that much could be achieved in reducing teenage fertility rates by increasing knowledge about sexual matters and contraception.

Contraceptive use at first intercourse has clear predictive value in relation to subsequent contraceptive competence and occurrence of teenage birth. Early education in the use of effective contraception, before the onset of sexual experience, could therefore be expected to influence contraceptive practice and impact on unintended fertility.

Improving communication

There is ample evidence that first sexual experience may not be optimally timed for many young people, particularly women, who often express regret. The strong association between age at first intercourse and occurrence of teenage fertility, leads to the conclusion that sex education must focus on providing communicational and negotiation skills to enable young people to avoid sexual experience which is perceived to be premature.

The strong link between communication about sex in the family and teenage birth underlines the importance of an easy environment in which to discuss sex. The means by which discussion might be facilitated should be made available to parents via educational materials, use of the media etc.

Service provision

The possibility that the way in which early motherhood is socially regarded may compound the problems facing teenage mothers must be borne in mind when mounting interventions. Care must be taken in providing services which avoid judgmental or retributive stances since these attitudes may deter the uptake of essential services. Provision of ante-natal and child health services must be provided which are specially tailored to the needs of unsupported young mothers.

The fact that the poorer health status of women who had been teenage mothers seems to persist up to the most recent time period, and is apparently independent of behaviour with adverse consequences for health, such as smoking, gives cause for concern. Attention needs to be paid to ways of involving women who become mothers early in life in preventive health care, and in providing them with means of support and stress management.

Encouraging educational attainment

The factor most strongly associated with teenage birth is that of educational attainment. Since lack of qualifications will compound the barriers to employment resulting from difficulties of child care and of balancing responsibility for early motherhood and work, more flexible arrangements for the pursuit of educational qualifications need to be widespread to ensure that teenage birth does not lead to further diminution of life chances.

Targeting young men

The disparity between prevalence estimates for teenage fatherhood and motherhood suggests that many young fathers may be unaware of, or may choose to disregard, the fact of their paternity. Young men may therefore constitute an important focus for efforts in this area of prevention.

Notes

1. The results reported in this chapter are expressed as median ages. This measure is given in preference to the mean (or average) because it is not affected by the extreme values, of which there are many in the area of sexual behaviour.

2. Sixteen is the legal age of sexual consent in England and the age a woman must reach for a man to be acting legally if he has sexual intercourse with her. In Scotland it is 17.

3. In the survey 'sexual experience' was defined as 'any type of experience of a sexual kind — for example, kissing, cuddling, petting — with someone of the opposite sex'.

4. Participants were asked to list all the methods they used in the past year, so more than one method may be reported per respondent.

References

1. Wellings, K., Field, J., Johnson, A.M. and Wadsworth, J. (1994), *Sexual Behaviour in Britain*. London: Penguin Publications.

2. Kinsey, A.C., Pomeroy, W.B. and Martin, C.E. (1948), *Sexual Behaviour in the Human Male*. Philadelphia; Saunders.

3. Kinsey, A.C., Pomeroy, W.B., Martin, C.E. and Gebhard, P.H. (1953), *Sexual Behaviour in the Human Female*. Philadelphia; Saunders.

4. Farrell, C. (1978), *My mother said ... the way young people learn about sex and birth*. Routledge and Kegan Paul. London.

5. Coles, R. and Stokes, G. (1985), *Sex and the American teenager*. New York, Harper and Row.

6. Fleissig, A. (1991), *Unintended pregnancies and the use of contraception: changes from 1984–1989*. British Medical Journal 302:147.

7. Holland, J. *et al.* (1990), *Sex, gender and power: young women's sexuality in the shadow of AIDS*. Sociology of Health and Illness 12(3): 336–350.

8. Skinner, C. (1986), *Elusive Mr. Right*. London: Carolina Publications.

9. Mellanby, A.R., Phelps, F., Lawrence, C. and Tripp, J.H. (1992), *Teenagers and the risk of sexually transmitted diseases: a need for balanced information*. Genitourinary Medicine 68:241–244.

10. Wellings, K. *et al.* (1996), *Teenage sexuality, fertility and life chances*. Report for the Department of Health.

11. Simms, M. and Smith, C. (1986), *Teenage Mothers and their Partners*. London, HMSO.

12. Moore, K. and Petersen, J. (1989), *The consequences of teenage pregnancy*. Final Report Washington DC. Child Trends, Inc.

13. Carlson, D., Labarba, R.C., Sclafani, J. D. and Bowers, C.A. (1986), *Cognitive and motor development in infants of adolescent mothers: a longitudinal analysis*. International Journal of Behavioural Development 9(1): 1–14.

14. Graham, H. (1987), *Women's smoking and family health*, Soc. Sci. Med., 25(1): 47–56.

15. Russell, J.K. (1988), *Early teenage pregnancy*. Maternal and Child Health Feb; 13(2): 43–6.

16. Macintyre, S. and Cunningham-Burley, S. (1993), *Teenage pregnancy as a social problem: a perspective from the United Kingdom*. In: The politics of pregnancy: adolescent sexuality and public policy, Annette Lawson and Deborah L. Phode (Eds.). New Haven, Connecticut, Yale University Press: 74–97.

SIX

Accentuating the Positive: HIV/AIDS and STDs Prevention and Education

Anne Mitchell

If you were an anxious parent or teacher any time before the 1970s, and were seeking some form of academic support for teaching the young people in your charge something to prepare them for the conflicts and decisions of their sexual development, your average bookshop might not have been of much help. You may have been directed to a medical text book retailer, the landslide of "how to parent" books, which was perhaps just beginning, remaining silent on this notoriously difficult subject. What you might have found would be predominantly scientific, focussing on plumbing and malfunction. Illustrations would have been obfuscated against any charge of obscenity by the inclusion of a breath-taking complexity of organs and systems to guide your interest away from the prurient. The author would most likely have been a gentleman of senior years and considerable eminence, this latter point staunchly evidenced by a list of medical qualifications which might also, in the best case scenario, include reference to a dabble in theology. Things to be prevented would almost certainly include masturbation and other less specified forms of moral degeneration which might lead to the (probably unspoken) consequences of conceiving a child out of wedlock or to infection with a blessedly short list of STDs.

The explosion of advice and opinions as to the "who, what, where and how" of sex education for the young is a relatively new phenomena. It parallels the growth of the World Health Organisation (WHO), the new discipline of health promotion, the blurring of distinctions between public and private, the growth of the so-called "permissive society" and shifts in the configuration of feared STDs. It owes as least as much to developments in popular culture as it does to those in pedagogy. Its relatively short history means that clear movements from darkness into light are yet to be distinguished, and that all the elements there at the beginning persist in some form still, increasing the contention around what is proper, useful and appropriate in the field. While older people may be allowed to decide for themselves the framework and values within which sexual behaviour is considered and takes place, extending this privilege to young people provokes great societal fear.

The advent of HIV, at present an incurable and potentially life-threatening disease has done much to ensure that sex education of some kind remains on the agenda, but little to clarify the kind of sex education that it might be. The most significant impact of HIV on sexuality education has been to confirm it's place in the health sphere in which moral imperatives must take second place. The consequences of backsliding became seen much more as death and disease rather than the shame, disgrace and moral damnation of earlier writing on the subject. Concerns about giving young people some glimmer of how babies are made or instruction to manage on the wedding night have been made redundant by shifts in social mores and popular culture. Young people can now garner such information from the public domain at will. The experts now are health professionals rather than parents and church leaders, and the new breed of medically-grounded health promotion professionals dedicated to achieving behaviour change. The current aim of this push for behaviour change is to preserve the sexual health of the young person, keeping them disease free and, as a secondary aim, without unintended pregnancy. It is becoming clear that in order to achieve such an aim, the scope of such programs needs to be continually broadened. Teachers and others who have professional contact with young people are required to adapt to this shift.

The issue of whether or not young people need sexuality education, revolving as it does around perceived degrees of risk to their well-being, has traditionally been dogged by a lack of universally acceptable documentation of such risk. The current collection of data relating to rates of HIV infection is well-developed world wide and able to demonstrate that in many countries young people may indeed risk their lives as a result of their sexual behaviour. It does however provide only a limited view of the real spectrum of risk. Data on STDs in young people is notoriously under reported and inconsistently recorded and so generally fails to provide solid evidence to support anecdotal reports from the medical profession that diseases other than HIV, some of them with very serious consequences, pose a far more common risk to young people. Research evidence for a continuing need for STD prevention education is better drawn from the large number of studies which indicate high levels of sexual activity and that many young people are continuing to practise unsafe sex regardless of any threats to their health.

This chapter will examine the conflict between the provision of information as opposed to more comprehensive education through evolving notions of which approaches have been seen to be most beneficial for achieving behaviour change in young people Secondly, the question of who the educators should be will be addressed. Evaluation of different current approaches to sexuality education will then be canvassed in relation to the question of what works and what does not. Finally, the chapter will seek to distil from the body of research available some of the key elements that may be useful in the education programs of the future.

Information or education?

The conflict between withholding or supplying information on sexual behaviour to young people in an educational setting, despite the fact that they now have many other sources for such information, persists to some extent. Fears remain that providing young people with information about contraception, oral and anal sex, or homosexual culture will instantly result in their increased activity on all fronts. This has particularly hampered provision of suitable resources and of many innovative programs in schools despite the fact that research indicates the opposite is likely to be true.

The solution to the dilemma has often been the provision of information in a context which makes sexual behaviour seem dangerous and unpalatable with a view to curbing the mindless hedonism of the young. It is probable that teaching with a focus on disease, disability, moral degeneracy, loss of reputation and social standing and other negative outcomes will have less appeal to young people than a holistic approach focussing on the positive.[1] Education based on fear and disapproval can present a view of sexuality which is so remote from the intense emotional longings and desires of the day to day reality of young people, that it must be challenged or discarded. Popular magazines are more likely to reflect this reality and so be seen, understandably, to have greater educational authority. Teaching for a more positive attitude to sexual development, leaving aside the matter of sexual enjoyment, at the most basic common sense level is more likely to lead to an improved commitment in young people to maintaining sexual health.

The new social model of health has much to offer the field of sexual health education. This model evolved out of the 1946 WHO holistic definition of health as more than the absence of disease, and the 1986 Ottawa Charter for Health Promotion which sees health as a more holistic state of being dependant and interwoven with the social, political and economic circumstances of the individual. In line with this WHO defines sexual health as:

"the capacity to enjoy and control sexual and reproductive behaviour in accordance with a social and personal ethic, freedom from fear, shame and guilt, false belief etc, which inhibit sexual responses and impair socio-sexual relationships, as well as freedom from organic disorders, disease and deficiencies that interfere with sexual and reproductive functions."

This broad-based definition recognises the wide range of factors that particularly impact on sexual behaviour, and the sense in which a positive capacity to enjoy sexual and reproductive potential is crucial to a concept of health.

Theories of health promotion for behaviour change have progressively recognised that simple provision of information about the negative consequences of an action will not bring about the required change, nor will a plea for rational decision-making.[2] The Health Belief Model, for example, which held that behaviour change arose out of knowledge about a disease, perceived susceptibility to the disease and perceived severity of the consequences of infection with the disease, has been tested in relation to HIV prevention and found wanting. It was found that while these factors were necessary elements of behaviour change in adolescents, they were not in themselves sufficient predictors of safe behaviour. The difficult and complex field of sexual behaviour has confounded approaches based on simple models of education for a particular end. Educators have been constantly left with a gap between what young people know and fear and what they will actually put into practice. Explaining and closing that gap has been the most recent challenge in STD prevention education. Knowledge alone about sexual and reproductive behaviour, about HIV and STDs, their transmission and their consequences appears to be a necessary, but insufficient precursor to behaviour change. Skills such as obtaining and effectively using condoms, or negotiating sexual encounters to ensure safety, are enhanced and strengthened by practice provided in education programs, but in and of themselves will not bring about the necessary changes in behaviour.

Theorists in HIV/AIDS education now acknowledge that, because sexual behaviour does not occur in a vacuum but is firmly embedded in a social and cultural context, information and skills practice provided without reference to this context will be meaningless.[3] This broader approach to education, which incorporates elements of discourse analysis[4] sees all sexual behaviour and beliefs about sex roles as socially and culturally constructed. In order to challenge beliefs and behaviours that may put a young person at risk, programs arising from this theoretical position seek to address the ways in which the society, the peer group, the ethnic and popular culture which surround the individual foster and perpetuate particular behaviours. Thus one might challenge and discuss the homophobia which underlies widespread beliefs about what "sex" is, or should be. Hidden racism which may deny individuals of particular cultures access to contraception or STD treatment may be exposed and addressed. Discussion of the impact of popular music or magazines on developing peer group beliefs about what is acceptable and "cool" may be considered with other ways of developing critical insight into peer group norms. These approaches offer at present a potential solution to the dilemma acknowledged by many who work with young people that information alone does not yield results.

This socially broader approach has particular relevance to addressing the issue of gender and the unequal power relations which exist in heterosexual encounters. The social environment in which the young person operates presents them continually with images and reinforcements of expectations about the role of young women and the role of young men, particularly in the sexual sphere. These expectations give rise to difficulties in sexual negotiations, diffidence about safe sex and condom use and the myriad of issues surrounding fear of loss of reputation in young women, as opposed to the less censured young men. Education remains one of the few means we have of challenging the historically dominant view that all sexuality is heterosexual, male and penis-defined, potentially reproductive and with equal power given to all players.[5] This challenging needs to address the broader social and cultural aspects of young women's lives and seek in particular to open discussion of their desires and longings, giving them the legitimacy of articulation.[6] Such articulation is a necessary precursor to exploring safe sex options which match the reality and not the expectations in their lives. This challenge to dominant social attitudes will inevitably work to benefit young men as well in potentially freeing them from expectations which may reduce their capacity to express fears and emotions within relationships. Aiming to create a space for young people in which they are supported to examine the impact of these expectations on their lives is a significant and worthwhile aim for sexuality education.

A further dimension of sexuality education is that directed towards reducing homophobia and fostering an appreciation of difference, allowing young people to explore and experience feelings around sexual preference without fear of rejection or harassment. The aim of such education is not simply to increase "tolerance" of homosexuals or potential homosexuals, but to challenge perceptions of heterosexuality as a monolithic reality. The gaining of insight into the socially constructed nature of sexual roles and behaviours and the sense of a continuum of sexual identity along which an individual may move in a lifetime, is critical in assisting all young people to understand more about their behaviour and the potential for positive changes. A lack of this insight may restrict all same sex friendships for some individuals [7] and inhibit safe behaviour in opposite sex relationships by restrictive adherence to perceived masculine and feminine behaviour. More importantly, such education is a necessary precondition to opening space for explicit safe sex information for young gay men whose failure to tap into other sources of such information appears in many countries to be leading to increased levels of HIV infection in the age group. [8]

A final issue which also impacts on the content and nature of HIV and STD prevention programs revolves around beliefs as to the role and nature of the person doing the education. Should such an educator be someone who is seen to have custodial care over as yet immature young people and some responsibility to protect them from too much too soon sexually? This view of education is one which gives rise to the "just say no" approach and sees adults as enforcers of such a regime. The alternative is to see the young person as potentially a competent decision maker and the educator as a support person for this process. The young person is to be given information which they may choose to use or not without criticism. Evaluation of school-based programs which are discussed below accord little success to the former approach. However, this debate remains a current one which keeps alive the question of who is responsible for sex education.

Who should be the educators?

While considerable debate, both academic and popular, still takes place around the question of who should deliver sex education to young people, it is something of a red herring. Young people as they move into adolescence become increasingly unwilling to accept a single source of authority without question. Cognitively their capacity to canvass different points of view and use them to form a personal opinion has increased markedly and the views of the peer group, however apparently ill-informed, may carry considerable weight against those of a doctor or teacher. This ranking of different points of view will reflect the needs and social beliefs of the young person in the here and now, and conventional beliefs around the primary importance of health and morality may be a casualty of the process. While this process offers very poor prospects of success for those who wish young people to hear and internalise only one point of view, it offers much that can be seen as positive. It means that everyone who has contact with young people may be engaged in some form of sexuality education and that there are many opportunities, however small, to assist young people to manage their developing sexuality well.

There is a popular perception in the current climate that parents, church leaders and other authority figures may be passing on values and morality around sexual behaviour while schools and medical people may offer "value-free" information. Popular culture sources, such as magazines and TV shows, may be perceived to offer information which is "cool" and "relevant", not pushing a point of view alien to the young person. In fact, it is often the case that the value systems and agendas underlying supposedly "value-free" messages, because they are hidden, present more confusion to the young person than a clearly moral perspective. This has been particularly demonstrated with the media [9] which young people regard as a favoured and accessible source of information. An example of such hidden values can be seen in the presumptive heterosexuality which underlies many sexuality-related resources and programs. By it's very existence, it is able to marginalise and discount the experience of many young people questioning and exploring their sexual orientation.

Those who have strong moral values around sexual behaviour are not necessarily inappropriate educators. Many parents, but by no means all, are in this category. There are a myriad of reasons why parents shy away from offering information and advice to their children about sexual behaviour. They may find the subject too hard or too embarrassing and so choose to back away from it and in doing so inevitably give their children messages which help to inform decision making. Unhappily, these are not necessarily the messages parents might wish to give. Barriers to broaching the subject may also include fears that the children may already know more than the parents, fear of having one's own values ridiculed and an unwillingness to accept that the child is growing into a sexually mature person. Research shows however that many young people see their parents as potentially reliable sources of information and support and do not feel they are getting as much from them as they would like.[10,11] Parents may never be a primary or sole source of information and education for young people, but they can feed sensitively into the process of developing a personal set of values by expressing their own views rather than attempting to enforce them, and by encouraging more open discussion when the occasion arises for young people.

The peer group plays a major role in influencing the behaviour of young people as they move more from accepting a single authoritative interpretation of the world to conceiving themselves as emergent adults seeking support and approval from others in the same situation. The power of peer influence has long been recognised by health promoters and has been documented as influential in the area of sexual behaviour.[12] Studies show that young people find peers a very accessible source of information and, even when they are seen as less reliable, they may use them in preference to approaching more traditional sources of information such as parents, teachers and doctors.[10] It would be remiss then to overlook the peer group as an important contributor to any sexual education program for young people and, although peer education programs have not been widely evaluated, they appear to be successful and remain popular. Notions of peer education, what it is or should be, what it should aim to achieve and how it should be conducted are all the subject of some debate. The fact that the peer group remains a powerful influence in this area however is beyond dispute and any programs which improve the quality of the information available in the peer group and the degree of support for safe behaviours must be seen to be worthwhile.

There are many out-of-school opportunities for sexuality education and those who work with young people as health carers, counsellors, church leaders, housing workers, sports coaches and in a variety of other settings in fact do much opportunistic health promotion as it arises. This is often on a one to one basis when an issue becomes important for an individual. Such education has great value as it has the dual advantage of coming from a trusted source chosen by the young person concerned, and of being offered at a time when an acute need can make the message more real.

Nevertheless, if one were to select an environment in which sexuality education can be most appropriately carried out, the school would have much to recommend it above the others. Kirby[13] points out that the majority of young people spend at least some part of their adolescence in school, and that schools are set up as the traditional sites of educational activity. While schools have the drawback of needing to teach large and sometimes culturally diverse groups all in the same way, they present an opportunity to offer some sexuality education for young people while they are still a captive audience. Many young people may never have access to this education again. Most of the evaluation of STD and HIV prevention education has been carried out in schools as a result of the large number of resources that have gone into such programs in the last decade. Evaluation is expedited by the definable nature of school programs and the fact that the students generally remain available in the system for some sort of post-program testing. For these reasons most of the data available about what sort of sexuality education is most successful are derived from schools. The search for answers as to what makes for good and effective sex education, has to be answered from these data.

What works? what doesn't?

It is important not to imply that the comparative ease of school-based program evaluation, makes such an undertaking clear cut or easy. The effectiveness of a program designed to bring about behaviour change is almost impossible to test. While it is possible to establish that most adolescents have a good knowledge base regarding HIV transmission,[14] it is difficult to prove the contribution of school programs to this knowledge. In fact, the spectacular discrepancy in high levels of knowledge about HIV and poor levels of knowledge about other STDs[15] may indicate that media attention to HIV in particular is as educative as programs in schools.

This underlines the impossibility of measuring a phenomena like risk-taking behaviour which is so embedded in developmental and social circumstances that the impact of any one thing cannot be determined. Kirby[16] points out that we do not subject other school-based education programs to the expectation that they will, in themselves, achieve behaviour change in young people outside school. In fact the achievement of higher levels of knowledge is generally deemed sufficient proof of success. He cautions about expecting too much of sexuality education and so setting such programs up for failure against impossibly unrealistic objectives. This may be of cold comfort to those operating in a climate of economic rationalism in which such accountability is demanded as a matter of course. His review of the effectiveness of school based programs commissioned by the Division of Adolescent and School Health within the Centre for Disease Control in the USA in 1993[17] reported the difficulties of making comparisons between a number of evaluation studies based on different indicators. The resultant study was able to assess comparatively twenty three studies which met a series of specified criteria and so draw some conclusions in this notoriously difficult field.

The study concluded that some elements of school programs did not seem to be relevant to either effective or ineffective programs. Length of program, the longest being the best, was not an assumption supported by this research. Skills development and practice was another component that was equally present in both effective and ineffective programs. Two elements of ineffective programs were able to be discerned, they were less focussed and more broad-based curriculum, and decision making models which gave students power to make their own decisions after learning the steps in a given model. Neither of these were seen to achieve the desired end. More importantly, some distinguishing characteristics of effective programs were able to be isolated. These were :

- a narrow focus on a few specific behavioural goals to reduce sexual risk taking
- using social learning theory as the basis of a program (social learning theory recognises the extent to which young people learn from role models and take on behaviours to emulate those they respect. This approach has been shown to be effective in reducing other risk behaviours.)
- providing basic accurate risk related and risk prevention information through experiential means with a capacity to personalise the information.
- inclusion of activities to address the power of social and media influences in this area.
- the strengthening of individual and group norms against unprotected sex through the reiteration of clear and appropriate values
- the use of peer education
- modelling and practice in communication and negotiation skills

Also emerging from this study was evidence that schools based programs did not increase the levels of sexual activity or hasten its onset. This finding was confirmed by Baldo *et al.*[18] who also found some evidence that such programs delayed the initiation of sexual activity. Kirby also concludes in his evaluation that there is no evidence to suggest that school-based programs advocating abstinence delay the onset of sexual activity or reduce teenage pregnancy rates.

It must be made clear that these elements which can be seen to be successful have emerged only as a result of particular programs which have been evaluated within very specific criteria. Frequently the aims of the programs will be so diverse as to make comparative evaluation meaningless. An evaluation of differently constructed more relationship based programs in Germany[19] indicated young people saw sex as increasingly linked to love and commitment so indicating the success of the program. Kirby[13] in another evaluation of schools programs points to the success of programs based on a "social influence model". These programs were based on theoretical models which acknowledged the impact of social contexts on young people's behaviour and, as such, had demonstrably more impact on behaviour change.

What are the implications for educators in the future?

It is difficult to use research and evaluation alone to determine what sexuality education will best meet the needs of a given group of young people. There is still insufficient data available to be able to draw up the blueprint for bringing about behaviour change, and a clear need for acknowledgement of the multiplicity of factors that operate outside the reach of any educational program. In addition, education in this area is still the subject of great debate and anxiety in many quarters and to do something remains better than to do nothing at all. It can be challenge enough to a school, community or institution to permit any program to operate, let alone an optimal one if such a notion were possible. It is important for all educators to be reconciled to the process of small incremental gains both in the climate which permits the education and in those young people who receive it. It is not an area where large

and immediate returns are likely to be evident and such indicators as an improved willingness in young people to ask questions,
or more open discussion between men and women about sexual
encounters can be very satisfactory evidence of success.

Educators need to appreciate that their role is one of feeding
into, not pre-empting, decision making. There is little to be gained
from imposing a single view of how a young person should think
and behave in relation to sexual matters. Developmentally the
moment for such an approach has passed. Just as we allow young
people to be licensed to drive with very little experience, acknowledging that in some cases harm will come of it, we must allow
young people to take control of their sexual development on the
understanding that by far the majority of them will make responsible decisions and manage well. Education can most effectively
enhance the process of emergent adult decision-making styles by
offering support for this process. Moral views and values are not
out of place at all, and form a vital and helpful part of the process
provided they are offered rather than imposed.

Information is essential, including the opportunity to ask questions
safely and pursue individual concerns. In line with good practice
principles of adult education, the best way to provide information
may be to direct the young person to resources such as books,
videos, a good health service where they can seek it out for themselves.
Tied in with these processes is the importance of offering safety,
privacy and confidentiality to young people while they are working the
issues through. Discussion needs to take place in a safe environment
with some protection for those who choose to disclose personal
information. Privacy is particularly important if a young person is
seeking advice on a specific health problem and this is an area
where parents and peers may not be the chosen sources of inquiry.
Health services in particular need to address this issue in their practices
to ensure young people can be assisted without their privacy being
violated or without recourse to their parents. Much debate has taken
place about the provision of school health clinics and designated
youth health services. An issue of critical importance for such services

will always be confidentiality, which is heightened when the presenting problem is a sexual one. General, rather than special purpose clinics offer enhanced protection to young people, as do organisations which offer more than medical services.

It is essential to bear in mind that by far the majority of young people manage their sexual development successfully and responsibly and it is needlessly destructive to begin without some optimism that this will be the case. HIV and STD prevention education must move away from a focus on death, disease, shame and other negative consequences of sexual behaviour. To educate in this way is to educate against the tide of adolescent development and the positive aspects of growth into adulthood, of which enjoying sexual feelings and experiences is one. Focussing on and decrying risk-taking behaviours (many of which may in themselves be positive indications of growth) is likely to be less effective than focussing on and valuing sexual development for itself. By this means young people may come to value their own health and take responsibility for maintaining it. Sexuality must be seen as a thing worth nurturing rather than something which is likely to be their undoing before they turn twenty one and can suddenly manage it.

Tied in with this is the importance of working from a broader definition of sexual health than the simple absence of STD infection or unintended pregnancy. Young people need to be encouraged to see relationships, feelings, desires, social acceptance and respect for others as part of their developing sexual persona, and as matters worthy of discussion and consideration in an educational context. An understanding of the impact of all these things on the individual is an essential prerequisite for those engaged in sexuality education.

This leads to an appreciation of the importance of education addressing the context. HIV and STD prevention education will not be successful unless it takes account of the cultural environment in which both education and sexual behaviour occur. Without this it is intervening in only a small area of the young person's life and offering no help or support with the more compelling factors which determine sexual beliefs. This may involve an awareness of the ethnic or religious background of members of the group, an appreciation of youth culture, popular culture or peer pressures. These issues must be brought into the classroom and become part of the critical awareness of young people before they can make decisions which take account of the complex reality of their lives. Paying critical attention to popular culture sources such as media and television can be a particularly useful way into the broader cultural context of sexual behaviour.

Acknowledging the broader social context will lead inevitably to teaching for sexual diversity and difference. This is not simply a matter of acknowledging that some young people may experience attraction to members of the same sex or to members of both sexes, but teaching in a way that ensures they have permission to do so. By opening up an appreciation of difference and challenging some of the fears that lead to homophobia and social rejection for some young people, broader aims can be achieved. These should include an enhanced understanding of young people who choose abstinence from sexual activity, perhaps against the peer group norm. The cultural or religious differences that underpin different experiences of sexual development can be as inhibiting as the experience of sexual preferences which run against the perceived norm. Norms are powerful tools for social control, they inhibit young women and young men and deny the reality of many individuals. They are barriers to the experience of sexual feelings as positive and unthreatening. Education which can address this issue will do much to prevent harm

The touchstone of all STD and HIV prevention should be harm minimisation. This approach seeks to offer support and assistance to the young person at any point to ensure they come to as little harm as possible. While the most desirable situation may be that the young person does not engage in any risky behaviour, it is not likely to be so for a large majority of young people. The most important thing is not to attempt to stop the behaviour through disapproval and chastisement which may increase feelings of guilt and hopelessness, but to ride out these aspects of adolescent behaviour by offering information and support to minimise harm. The clearest example of this approach is the provision of condoms and information about using them to young people so that if they choose to have sexual intercourse at some stage they are prepared and informed about the safest options. In the area of drug use, the ideal is that young people do not use drugs. However, as some will inevitably do so, it is better that they be discouraged from intravenous use or provided with clean injecting equipment than to be needlessly exposed to infection. Research has indicated that cities with a well-established needle and syringe exchange program have been far more successful in minimising infection amongst the intravenous drug using population than those which have had no such intervention.[20]

Even young people who are not engaging in risky behaviour may, under social or emotional pressures, choose to do so at some point. At the very least it is important that they have foreknowledge of the means to limit harm, and ideally freedom from the feelings of shame and negativity which may make them feel being prepared with condoms or clean needles is a sign of moral degeneracy. To this end, the use of non-judgemental matter of fact language in sexuality education contributes to a harm minimisation approach. Avoiding words with a moral or perjorative tone such as "addict", "promiscuous", "premarital" and "unfeminine" will prevent alienating the young person from the essential health message. The essential health message is a parachute we wish them to have in a crisis while goals which involve the disengagement from all health risks may be more long-term.

Education will be most successful if it comes from an appreciation of where the young person is focussed at any given time, the things they value most in their lives and the context in which they operate. It needs to be based on a belief that every young person is making choices about their lives on evidence they regard as compelling, and to seek to feed into this process to optimise the health outcomes for every individual.

References

1. Tones, B.K (1986), "Health education and the ideology of health promotion: a review of alternative approaches" *Health Education Research*, 1(1): 3–12.

2. Ingham, R. Woodcock, A. and Stenner, K. (1991), "Getting to know you ... young people's knowledge of their partners at first intercourse" *Journal of Community and Applied Psychology* 1: 117–32.

3. Parker, R. (1994), "Sexual cultures, HIV transmission and AIDS prevention" *AIDS*, 8 (suppl.), S309–314.

4. Potter, J. and Wetherall, M. (1987), *Discourse and Social Psychology: Beyond Attitudes and Behaviour* (London: Sage).

5. Mac An Ghaill, M. (1996), "Deconstruting heterosexualities within school arenas" *Curriculum Studies*, 4(2)

6. Fine, M.(1988), "Sexuality, schooling, and adolescent females: The missing discourse of desire" *Harvard Educational Review* 58: 29–53.

7. Crooks, R. and Baur, K. (1990), "Homosexuality" in *Our Sexuality* (California: Benjamin/Cummings).

8. Uribe, V. and Harbeck, K. (1992), "Addressing the needs of lesbian, gay and bisexual youth: The origins of PROJECT 10 and school-based intervention" in K.M. Harbeck (ed.) *Coming Out of the Classroom Closet: Gay and Lesbian Students, Teachers and Curricula* (New York: The Harvard Press).

9. McRobbie, A. (1991), *From 'Jackie' to 'Just Seventeen'* (London: Macmillan).

10. Rosenthal, D.A. and Smith, A.M.A. "Adolescents and sexually transmitted diseases: Information sources, preferences and trust" *Health Promotion Journal of Australia*, in press.

11. Rosenthal, D.A. and Collis, F. "Parents' beliefs about adolescent sexuality and HIV/AIDS" *Journal of HIV Education and Prevention in Children and Adolescents*, in press.

12. Irwin, C.E. Jr. and Millstein, S.G. (1986), "Biopsychosocial correlates of risk-taking behaviours during adolsecence" *Journal of Adolescent Health Care* 7: 82–96.

13. Kirby, D. (1992), "School-based prevention programs: Design, evaluation, and effectiveness" in DiClemente, R.J. (ed.) Adolescents and AIDS: *A Generation in Jeopardy*, (Newbury Park, CA: Sage).

14. Anderson, M.D. and Christenson, G.M. (1991), "Ethnic breakdown of AIDS-related knowledge and

attitudes from the National Adolescent Student Health Survey" *Journal of Health Education* 22: 30–4.

15. Smith, A.M.A, Rosenthal, D.A. and Tesoriero, A. (1995), "Adolescents and sexually transmissible diseases: Patterns of knowledge in Victorian high schools" *Venereology* 8: 83–8.

16. Kirby, D. (1995), "Sexuality Education: A more realistic view of its effects" *Journal of School Health* 55 (10): 421–424.

17. Kirby, D., Short, L., Collins, J. Rugg, D., Kolbe, L., Howard, M., Miller, B , Sonenstein, F. and Zabin, L. (1994), "School-based programs to reduce sexual risk behaviours: A review of effectiveness" *Public Health Reports* 109:339–60.

18. Baldo, M., Aggeleton, P. and Slutkin, G. (1993), *Sex Education Does Not Lead to Earlier or Increased Sexual Activity in Youth*, Report to the World Health Organisation Global Program on AIDS Geneva, Switzerland.

19. Schmidt, G., Klusmann, D., Zeitzschel, U. and Lange, C. (1994), "Changes in adolescents' sexuality between 1970 and 1990 in West Germany" *Archives of Sexual Behaviour* 23: 489–513.

20. Wodak, A. (1995), "Needle exchange and bleach distribution programmes: The Australian experience" *The International Journal of Drug Policy* 6: 46–57.

SEVEN

Strategies for Preventing Unplanned Pregnancies

Isobel Allen

"One of the great challenges for service providers and those working with young people
is to design services which meet young people's needs and are attractive enough for
them to use them regularly and consistently."[1]

This sentence is taken from *Family Planning and Pregnancy Counselling
Projects for Young People*, an evaluation carried out by Policy Studies
Institute of three projects set up with Department of Health funding
which had the twin aims of reducing the risk of unwanted pregnancies
among young people and of encouraging them to seek advice early
if they suspected they were pregnant. Much of the evidence presented
in this chapter is based on this evaluation, although it draws on the
author's previous and subsequent research on family planning and
related services, teenage pregnancies, and education in sex and
personal relationships (see references). It also draws on the extensive
body of research over the past 20 years related to strategies for
preventing unplanned pregnancies, which mainly cover two broad
areas: (i) education programmes designed to reduce the incidence of
unintended teenage pregnancies; and (ii) the delivery of contraceptive
and counselling services with the same aim.

The focus of this chapter will be on the second broad area — the
delivery of contraceptive and counselling services designed to reduce
the incidence of unintended teenage pregnancies — since other chapters in this book are looking at issues around sex education policies.
However, it is important to stress that all good contraceptive and
counselling services will include a strong element of education within
their remit, and there is little doubt that this element is particularly
important in services designed specifically for teenagers.

There is a clear need for coordinated strategies to help prevent unintended teenage pregnancies. The most recent international figures show that England and Wales had the highest fertility rates among 15–19 year olds in Europe[2] — nearly five times those in the Netherlands — although rates in the United States were considerably higher. The latest figures for England and Wales[3] show that the vast majority — 92 per cent — of the 85,000 teenagers who became pregnant in 1994 were unmarried and 35 per cent of them had an abortion. 7,800 girls under the age of 16 became pregnant and just over half of their pregnancies — 4,100 — were ended by abortion. Although teenage conception rates have fallen in England and Wales since the early 1970s,[4] they still have a long way to go to match those of other European countries.

Background to the young people's projects

The Department of Health set up the three young people's projects in 1987 because research funded by the Department[5,6] had suggested that the needs of younger people were not being adequately met by existing provision for family planning and abortion. The Department of Health stressed that its own policy for many years had been to encourage health authorities to consider establishing separate facilities for the young. Evidence at the time suggested that only 50 per cent of health authorities actually had such facilities.[7] By 1991 it was estimated that 56 per cent of health authorities had young people's contraceptive clinics, whereas by 1995 the proportion had increased to as many as 85 per cent of health authorities.[8]

The three young people's projects were set up in the health districts of City and Hackney, Milton Keynes and South Sefton with Department of Health funding. The original intention had been for them to be funded for a three year period, but in the event the funding covered an eighteen-month period from October 1987 to March 1989. Policy Studies Institute was asked to evaluate the work of the projects. Essentially the three projects were set up as 'demonstration' projects and one of the main aims was to see to what extent they could be used as 'models' for others who might want to initiate or develop family planning and pregnancy counselling services for young people.

This chapter examines three main areas of the evaluation: first, the organisation and staffing of the projects; secondly, some of the main findings both about the 'direct' services provided by the projects — the clinic and drop-in services — and the outreach work undertaken by the projects; and thirdly, the views and experience of young people themselves, including their experience of sex education. This analysis is put in the context of other research carried out by the author on education in sex and personal relationships among teenagers and on work roles and responsibilities in GUM clinics. The final section of the chapter highlights some of the conclusions and recommendations from the evaluation of the young people's projects, which were quoted in full in the 1992 guidelines issued to health authorities for reviewing family planning services by the NHS Management Executive.[9]

The projects and their problems

In all three areas, the projects were set up to provide both a direct contraceptive and pregnancy counselling service to young people and to develop outreach work with young people and other professionals and agencies. In Milton Keynes and South Sefton, the projects provided a direct service to young people at their project base through a daily drop-in service and a weekly clinic session with a doctor present. Both these clinic sessions took place in the early afternoon. Both projects aimed to develop outreach work with young people and other professionals and agencies from their project base. The same staff were responsible for both the direct service and the outreach work, with the additional help of a clinic doctor only for the clinic session. In City and Hackney, a quite different model was set up, with the direct service to young people being provided by Brook Advisory Centres at three clinic sessions based in a health centre on two evenings a week and a Saturday morning. The outreach work with young people and professionals was provided by the City and Hackney Young People's Project (CHYPP) team from their base in the district community health headquarters. There was no drop-in service: Brook provided a clinic service, and the CHYPP team provided outreach services only. The CHYPP team was available for consultation by telephone basically only to professionals, and received only a handful of telephone calls from young people during the monitoring period.

In terms of staffing, CHYPP had a full-time coordinator and one full-time and two part-time development workers. The Brook clinic staff was usually made up of an administrator, a doctor, a nurse and a lay counsellor at each session. In Milton Keynes, there were originally four health workers, two of whom had previously been employed in a Women's Health Group based in the same premises used by the project. In South Sefton, there were two health workers and a clerical/administrative officer. In Milton Keynes and South Sefton the clinic doctors were local women GPs. Most of the staff were in their thirties and forties, and only one team member and one doctor were under thirty. Only one male worker was employed on any of the projects, although Brook sometimes employed male doctors in City and Hackney.

The evaluation

The Policy Studies Institute evaluation concentrated on who used the project services, what they got, who provided it, and what the users — both young people and professionals — thought of the services provided by the projects.

This approach demanded a number of different research methods, which are discussed in detail in the book.[10] Briefly, we closely monitored the activities of the projects and, in addition, we carried out a series of interviews — with the project teams and their managers and advisers at the beginning and end of the monitoring period, with 110 professionals working with young people in the districts towards the end of the monitoring period, with 142 young people using the project premises in Milton Keynes and South Sefton and the Brook clinic in City and Hackney, and with 31 young women who had not used the projects, the majority of whom had had an unwanted pregnancy.

Main findings about the direct services

The projects were strikingly different from each other in the numbers of people and the type of clientele they attracted to their direct services, which was interesting because Milton Keynes and South Sefton offered essentially the same type of service — a drop-in centre open every day and a weekly clinic. City and Hackney offered a clinic service through Brook three times a week, and no drop-in service. In terms of population reached, 883 people (876 women and 7 men) made at least one visit to the City and Hackney Brook clinic in the 18-month period. The comparable figures for the Milton Keynes project were 711 people (701 women and 10 men), and for South Sefton 360 people (210 women and 150 men). But these statistics do not reveal the wide variation in the types of visit, service received and age of attender.

The City and Hackney Brook clinic tended to appeal to young women in their twenties rather than teenagers — 20 per cent of the users were over 25 and nearly 50 per cent were between 20 and 24. In the other two areas, the statistics were more complicated in that we distinguished between people who used the clinic only, the drop-in service only, and those who used both clinic and drop-in service. It was important to do this, because they were different types of clients coming for different types of reasons, but it made the analysis very complicated.

In Milton Keynes, the vast majority of users went to the drop-in services only and less than one fifth of the users went to the clinic at all. The clinic attenders tended to be younger than in the other two areas, with around one fifth under 16 and over half between 16 and 19. However, nearly half the users of the drop-in service were between 20 and 24. In South Sefton, over one third of the women users of the project were over 25, and over 40 per cent of the clinic users were over 25, with one-sixth being over 40. There were some doubts about whether the clinic could be called a young people's clinic at all, and there were certainly indications that the project itself was demonstrating a gap in service provision for all women in that area rather than a need for a young people's service only. One of the striking things about the South Sefton project was the extent to which they attracted young men. 150 young men came to the project, of whom 80 per cent were teenagers and over a fifth were schoolboys under the age of 16. They came for the free condoms, but they all saw a health worker, and nearly a fifth of them saw the clinic doctor. South Sefton certainly made a breakthrough in getting at the boys.

The major difference between the projects lay in the extent to which they were used as pregnancy counselling and pregnancy testing services.

- Nearly half the City and Hackney women had pregnancy tests at their first visit, most of which were positive, and the majority sought a termination of pregnancy.
- In Milton Keynes, nearly 90 per cent of women attending the drop-in service had a pregnancy test. Nearly half were positive, but the majority of these intended to continue with their pregnancy, and a further 10 per cent who had negative results wanted to be pregnant.
- In South Sefton, the picture was different again. It was much less often used for pregnancy testing, but over two-thirds of those tested were negative, of whom some wanted to be pregnant. On the other hand, it was used to quite a large extent as a well-woman clinic for women over the age of 25.

This sketch of the profile of users of the direct services shows not only how different the projects were from each other, but also how they did not really fall into the pattern of service provision for young people envisaged either by the Department of Health or by the health authorities when they were putting in their original bids for funding.

The young people

We were interested in what young people themselves wanted, particularly in what teenagers wanted. We interviewed those using the clinics and drop-in services — and some who had not used the services.

What did they want? They wanted a lot of local centres, which were discreet and inconspicuous, but easy to find and well-publicised. They wanted them to be open at convenient times, to be informal and non-clinical, staffed by friendly, non-judgmental, well-qualified staff who made them feel comfortable and did not tell them off. They wanted doctors who were kind and friendly, explained things well, gave them time and were not 'stern'. They did not want the staff to be 'grumpy old bags who think you're too young...' They expressed a need for services offering general counselling on problems which might affect all teenagers. Above all they wanted the services to be confidential at all levels.

One of the main findings was the need for publicity to young people, and the need to plug into their network so that they use the clinic or drop-in services of young people's projects *before* they become pregnant rather than after. Once the young people got to the projects they were usually very satisfied and pleasantly surprised at how they were treated and the kindness of the staff.

They particularly liked the doctors. Over 70 per cent of those interviewed said that what they liked was that the doctor was friendly and nice and relaxed, and they often seemed to have rather curious views of their own doctors. A 16 year old talking of the clinic doctor said: 'She was friendly. She didn't seem like a doctor. Doctors really lay into you — interrogate you...'

The use of the word 'friendly' in describing the project doctors was striking in these interviews with young women. There was certainly an image of doctors in general being rather formal, unfriendly, wearing white coats and sitting behind desks, which came through in these interviews time and again. The younger the girls the more they presented an image of their own doctors as being forbidding and disapproving. A 16 year old girl in South Sefton described what she liked about the clinic doctor: 'She didn't tell me what to do. She just advised me about what would be best for myself. And she never shouted at me. She never had a doctor's uniform on — a white coat. She looked comfortable...'

Very few women mentioned spontaneously that they liked seeing a woman doctor, although this is frequently mentioned as necessary by professionals or family planning clinic doctors. We asked the young women how much it mattered to them whether they saw a man or a woman doctor. They divided roughly into four groups, each representing around a quarter of the sample: those who would much prefer to see a woman; those who would prefer to see a woman but would not refuse to see a man; those who commented that women doctors were generally more sympathetic or understanding than men doctors, but were not prepared to state categorically that they preferred one or the other. And the last group said it did not matter what sex the doctor was, often adding that it was irrelevant as long as the doctor was good at his or her job and nice and friendly. There can be little doubt that friendliness goes a long way in making people think that a doctor is good.

Nearly half the young women said they felt nervous or worried about going to the project for the first time — and the younger they were the more nervous they were. Some thought they might be thought too young to go, even though the projects were advertised as being specifically for young people. A 17 year old said: 'I felt that I was bit too young. I thought they might think I was too young to be here...'

However, more than half the women were not worried about going to the projects, often because they had heard about the project from a friend or had actually been with a friend. As with so many of these services, the 'grapevine effect' is very important, which is one reason why it takes time for a new service to get established. But relying on the grapevine effect is clearly not enough, and time and again research reinforces the need for good, professional continuing publicity, combined with good relations with other professionals to help services of this kind get off the ground — and stay off the ground.

We were concerned that there was a lot of evidence that the images young people have of GPs — and family planning clinics — were not always favourable. GPs were seen as formal, unfriendly, stern and disapproving, and, most important, a lot of young people had severe doubts about the extent to which their consultations about family planning or unwanted pregnancies with their GPs would remain confidential. They were very worried that their GPs would tell their parents even if they were over 16.

Family planning clinics were often seen as places for 'older' people, frequently taken to be people over the age of 20. The name was puzzling for teenagers who were not planning families, let alone any other part of their lives. Teenagers in particular were pretty vague about family planning clinics, and often thought they were the same as infant welfare clinics. They were concerned about meeting people who might know their families, and thought there would be no disguising why they were there, unlike a doctor's waiting room.

However, relatively few of the young women interviewed had actually used a family planning clinic, and the younger they were the less likely they were to have used one. There was some evidence that young women had not always received much help if they had been to a family planning clinic in connection with an unwanted pregnancy. And it must be remembered that a high proportion of those using these projects for the first time were either pregnant or concerned that they might be pregnant.

It often seemed that many of the views about GPs and family planning clinics were based on images rather than reality. For example, the women doctors in Milton Keynes and South Sefton were local GPs, and there are many GPs of both sexes who work in family planning clinics. It seems very unlikely that they change character the minute they enter a clinic, and turn from being stern, formal and unfriendly people into being friendly, warm and sympathetic. We also think that there may be a breakdown in communications and that young people should be made aware of the fact that they do not necessarily have to be ill to engage the sympathy and help of their GPs.

We recommended the need both for clinic sessions with a doctor present and for a drop-in service with counselling, information and advice from non-medical personnel. Some young people have a lot of problems, while others need a friendly chat to help them sort out problems which might not need a medical input. But counsellors should be trained and knowledgeable, and not just a friendly ear. And clinic sessions should not take place in the early afternoon. It is not really desirable for girls to 'bunk off' school or take time off work to come to a clinic. It might be difficult to get GPs to come as clinic doctors later in the afternoon, but if the service is to attract teenagers, then it must fit in with their timetable.

Sex education

Most of the young people we interviewed had received education on sex, personal relationships and contraception at school, but most of them thought they had not received enough. Some thought they had received too little too late, some thought they had had too much too early, while others appeared to have missed it altogether because they had not been at school that day, or they had changed schools, or they were boys. In any case, having a lot of good sex education did not necessarily prevent pregnancies as many of our interviews both in this study and other studies have indicated. It is undoubtedly difficult for schools to get sex education right for everyone. Some people had been at the same schools in the same classes at the same time, but some had clearly taken everything in, while others had not noticed that they had had any sex education at all.

Everyone was sceptical about the value of the 'usual whispers' and 'snippets' of information they could glean from friends and contemporaries. Many had good relationships with parents, but did not always find it easy to talk to them about sex. Like young people interviewed in earlier Policy Studies Institute research,[11] they valued fairly structured discussion with members of the opposite sex in the context of a discussion group at school and they valued the input of experts. They were very keen that both boys and girls should have sex education and stressed that discussion of emotions and feelings were as important as information about the biological facts.

Main findings about outreach work

The outreach activities of the projects were very important, but demonstrated many of the difficulties encountered by projects of this kind. They were part of the strategic approach adopted by the projects in preventing unplanned pregnancies through trying to integrate educational programmes into their service delivery programmes, but met with varying degrees of success which have major lessons for others planning services.

The three projects all laid great store on the need to 'network' with other professionals and agencies working with young people, but they achieved mixed results, and there were a number of messages from this. In some instances not enough thought had been given at the planning stage to how relationships with existing family planning clinic staff would be handled, and there were instances of rather distant, not to say frosty, relationships between the projects and family planning staff. We did feel that this sense of rivalry was quite inappropriate and should have been ironed out before the projects began. Similarly, relationships with GPS and hospital staff (both medical and nursing), were almost non-existent, but we felt that there was an urgent need to develop these relationships. Young people need the services of a variety of professionals, and their needs are paramount — not the finer feelings of professionals.

The main success stories were with the schools, although in South Sefton there were continuing difficulties for the project team in gaining access to the Catholic schools. Milton Keynes was particularly successful in working with schools, both in terms of providing resources for the teachers and in terms of conducting sessions with the young people themselves. City and Hackney also had success with teachers, especially to begin with. City and Hackney worked well with residential social workers dealing with young people. None of the projects had much success with the youth service, and there were indications that they found it difficult to understand or penetrate the culture. There was success with some Youth Training Schemes — and evidence that this was an area in which there was a great need for activity of this kind. The CHYPP team from City and Hackney spent a lot of time developing a teenage ante-natal clinic which had been a relatively unsuccessful venture run by the health authority, and in supporting a post-natal clinic and a young mothers' group.

However, in all three areas we found a good deal of ignorance on the part of the professionals we interviewed of the activities of the projects, even if they had had contact with them, and there was little doubt that a lot of hard work and good publicity is needed to convince professionals and other agencies that young people's services are good places to which to refer young people.

It should be stressed that the study found a lot of evidence of very enlightened attitudes among those who were working with young people already, and we recommended that a two-way flow of information and thinking about the best ways of providing services for young people should be regarded as essential. Newcomers can bring fresh ideas and a new approach to services, but they should also be acutely aware of what is going on already, and work closely with people already in the field.

Outreach work should include both the resourcing and training of other professionals to provide sex education, and the offer of packages of sex education which young people's project workers can deliver themselves or can be delivered by professionals already working with young people. Young people's services have a major role to play in the area of education in sex and personal relationships, including HIV/AIDS education, and their expertise and resources should be utilised wherever possible. However, it is essential that any outreach work of an educational nature is carried out in close collaboration with the health education or health promotion department of the health authority, with the local education authority and with HIV/AIDS education officers or coordinators.

Summary of recommendations

In summarising the recommendations of the report, it is important to note that some of them were general in planning strategies for preventing unplanned pregnancies and some were addressed specifically to those providing the services. Young people need services providing family planning, pregnancy counselling, sex education, and, if there are specially designated services, they should be targeted at young people under the age of 20. They should have clear aims and objectives, should be given proper management support and guidelines and everybody should be informed of what they are there for. They should provide both direct and outreach services, as outlined in this chapter. Staffing, premises, opening hours and atmosphere are all crucially important, but the key consideration is ensuring confidentiality. This is of paramount importance to young people.

It is a good idea for the same staff to undertake both direct and indirect services if possible. Good, professional, continuing publicity is crucial — and the publicity should be aimed both at young people and at other professionals and agencies. Word of mouth publicity is important and every effort should be made to tap into the young people's 'grapevine'. Publicity should be available where young people go. Lessons should be learnt from the experience of other areas. It should not be necessary to reinvent the wheel every time a new young people's service is set up.

The management and planning of the services is very important, and good support services are essential. Liaison with other agencies is fundamental to the success of these services, and a good way of achieving this is through a multidisciplinary advisory group which has authority and credence.

Services should be properly monitored. There is no point in setting up a service without good records and monitoring systems already in place, through which effects and effectiveness can be demonstrated. Regular systematic evaluation of the data is essential, both for review and planning purposes.

People working in family planning clinics or young people's clinics should not assume that all GPs and hospital doctors are incapable of providing services to young people or that young people do not like them, just because they see the ones who may have had problems.

Similarly, GPs should not think they have the answer to everything and that family planning or young people's clinics or drop-in services are 'poaching' their patients. It is essential that young people have a choice. They will not use one service to the exclusion of all others for all their lives, and they need to feel secure in using medical services.

One of the main findings of the evaluation of the young people's projects — and other research carried out by Policy Studies Institute in the past and more recently — is that young people prefer one door to knock on at a time. They do not want to go from pillar to post for extra bits of service. This is why it is so important to try and provide help when it is asked for, wherever it is asked for. There is much to be said for providing other health-related and counselling services for young people at the same venue.

The provision of education in sex and personal relationships should be closely linked with education about HIV/AIDS and other sexually transmitted diseases. It is difficult to see how one can be delivered without the other, and there should be complete integration between the two strands. It seems to provide quite unnecessary duplication, with the danger of conflicting or confusing messages being delivered to vulnerable young people. They should not exist as two parallel programmes but there should be unified management and delivery of such programmes. Sexual health should be the main aim of all services and educational programmes.

There should be a continuing development of programmes of education in sex and personal relationships. There have been alarming indications in recent years that such programmes might be squeezed out with the demands of the national curriculum, the lessening influence and resources of local education authorities and the placing of responsibility for such programmes in the hands of school governors. It is difficult to see how the Health of the Nation targets[12] for the reduction in pregnancies among under-16 year olds can be achieved in the absence of good sex education at school. Although having sex education at school does not necessarily mean that young people do not get pregnant, there is plenty of evidence to suggest that it helps. But there certainly seems to be a need for constant monitoring and improving of sex education programmes.

Finally, in developing strategies for preventing unplanned pregnancies among teenagers, it must be remembered that new services take time to establish themselves. Instant success should not be expected, even if all the recommendations for developing young people's services outlined above are followed.

References

1. Allen, I. (1991), Family Planning and Pregnancy Counselling Projects for Young People. London: Policy Studies Institute.

2. Babb, P. (1993), Teenage conceptions and fertility in England and Wales, 1971–1991. Population Trends. Winter 1993. No.74: 12–17. London: HMSO.

3. Office for National Statistics (1996), Conceptions in England and Wales 1994. ONS Population and Health Monitor FM1, 1996/2.

4. Office for National Statistics (1996), Birth Statistics England and Wales. FM1 No.23 London: HMSO.

5. Allen, I. (1985), Counselling Services for Sterilisation, Vasectomy and Termination of Pregnancy. London: Policy Studies Institute.

6. Simms, M. and Smith, C. (1986), Teenage Mothers and their Partners. London: HMSO.

7. Family Planning Association (1985), District Health Authority Family Planning Services in England and Wales. London: FPA.

8. Brook Advisory Centres (1995), Brook Advisory Centres Annual Report. London: Brook Advisory Centres.

9. NHS Management Executive (1992), Guidelines for Reviewing Family Planning Services: Guidelines for Regions. London: Department of Health.

10. Allen (1991), *op.cit*

11. Allen, I. (1987), Education in Sex and Personal Relationships. London: Policy Studies Institute.

12. Department of Health (1992), Health of the Nation. London: HMSO.

EIGHT

Peer-Led Sex Education in the Classroom

APAUSE – Added Power and Understanding in Sex Education – a collaborative intervention between education, health and young people.

John Rees, Alex Mellanby and John Tripp

> "The world is in decay, the young no longer respect their elders."
> Stone Carving, China 2000 BC.

Introduction

The Health of the Nation[1] document explains that health and well-being can be partly attributed to good personal, social and, by implication, sexual relationships. Whatever their social or professional responsibilities, those concerned with promoting health are under increasing pressure to find effective strategies to combat the increasing problems faced by successive generations of adolescents. Existing, new and re-worked policies are being evaluated not only for their propensity for behaviour change but also for their cost effectiveness. Such strategies, especially in schools, are set in an increasingly challenging social context and at a time of restricted budgets. Johnson et al.[2] reported that the median age of first intercourse for men aged 16–19 was three years earlier than it was for those aged 55–59. Unwanted teenage pregnancy continues to be of great concern and the prevalence of Sexually Transmitted Diseases (STD's) in the under 19 population continues to rise. The chapter below outlines the process (and the theories on which it is based), the programme that we have developed for delivering effective sex education to young people in secondary school. This work was based on the APAUSE[3] project which is now moving from research to service mode and is operating in schools in Devon, North Essex and Teesside.

Sex in adolescence clearly is not, and never has been, without risks. These have become more relevant to an increasing number of adolescents in Britain during recent years. Adolescence is characterised by the initiation of intimate sexual relationships and a variety of other behaviours that may involve risks to their future health and development. Their bodies, social expectations and the demands from those around them, change with what must seem to be bewildering rapidity. Young people now have perhaps less chance than their predecessors of knowing what "goal posts" there are, let alone where they might be found or may have been, until the latest shift! For such reasons they are particularly vulnerable to the negative aspects of sexual risk taking such as unwanted pregnancy, STD's, infertility and the health and social complications associated with each of these.

As children grow from infancy to adolescence, so too does the influence that their peers have on their development. In all societies, the peer group inevitably influences both attitudes and behaviour, particularly as the individual achieves a greater independence from their family. The explanation for young people's preference for same age groupings in complex societies is probably due to the (generally) positive nature of that social interaction. It may be argued, that those best placed to help guide our young people through the turbulence of adolescence are their peers who have recently made such a journey. The challenge for society, educators and especially for health professionals is to invoke the 'Heineken principle': "How can we help our young people reach those parts of themselves that conventional education cannot reach?"

Peer education is not new; the 'monitorial system' was commonplace in elementary schools in England during the 1800s. Allen[4] suggests that the tutoring by older students to teach younger ones was more a matter of necessity than of educational philosophy. However, this provided an inexpensive method of delivering information to a large number of pupils. More recently, peer

educators have been used in a number of health promotion programmes including prevention of drug,[5] alcohol [6] and tobacco
misuse,[7] eating disorders and to ease the transition from primary
to secondary school.[8] Carr[9] reported that a search of the World-
Wide Web yielded 37,000 documents under a heading of "peer
work".

Despite the profusion of health-promoting projects who use
"peer" support, there is little consensus as to what constitutes a
peer programme. Sciacca[10] defines peer health education as: "... *the
teaching or sharing of health information, values and behaviours by
members of similar age or status groups.*" Jaquet *et al.*[11] develop this
with specific reference to young people, suggesting that peer education is: "... *an approach which empowers young people to work with
other young people, and which draws on the positive strength of the peer
group. By means of appropriate training and support, the young people
become active players in the educational process rather than passive recipi-
ents of a set message.*" They add that, central to this work, is the
collaboration by young people and adults. Some evidence indicates that pupils learn more in peer education settings than in the
more usual classroom context. Topping[12] goes as far as to say this
evidence is "incontrovertible". Although peer education has not
been common to all successful programmes identified by Kirby[13],
Fong[14] concludes that peer educators are probably an essential component in health programmes that demonstrate significant behavioural change.

Theoretical perspective

Without recourse to effective theory, sex education and other
health interventions may become reliant on delivering factual information. Some programmes become concerned with getting
through material, attempting for example to deal with *all* the
methods of contraception, *all* the sexually transmitted diseases
and *all* the ways to catch them or avoid them. Such teaching has
not been shown to result in young teenagers being less likely to

expose themselves to the vagaries of chance in conceiving or contracting disease. It may not even enable them to retain accurate knowledge. While it is not suggested that inaccuracy of factual sex education results in unsafe sexual activity, clearly information alone does not allow teenagers to take control of emotions and relationships. This is particularly true in activities which include that most powerful of human drives (to reproduce) and also are swayed by external pressures and unrealistic beliefs about activities that others are enjoying. It is unsurprising that cognitive based, adult derived, health education is not associated with a reduction in some of the outcomes that are unwanted by teenagers, or adults.

Regis[15] states what he describes as a consensus view that *"school's health education should be about promoting informed choice, perhaps even valuing the quality of decision over its content."* He goes on to quote Kolbe[16] who suggested that from this premise, *"turning a shallow, conformist non-smoker into an independent, rational and self-aware person who decides to smoke, may even be seen as a health education success."* We consider this supposed divide between 'education' and 'health' to be artificial. In keeping with any sophisticated society, teachers, medics and the young people themselves will support a radical stance centred on empowerment and choice rather than compliance and coercion. This is in the best interest of the young people we all seek to serve and support.

Although there is an apparent logic to Kolbe's statement, especially when considering programmes designed to counter substance misuse-use we refute this argument in the case of sex education. Arguably there is also a difference when peer educators are introduced as part of drugs education rather than when they contribute to a sex education programme. Social (adult) ambivalence to different forms of drug taking ranging through caffeine, alcohol and tobacco to marihuana to other illegal substances lends confusion to the experience of adolescents. Here the agenda will need to be negotiated between the health and education professionals with the peer educators. In sex education, there is less uncertainty. Unwelcome pressure, STD's (including HIV/AIDS), unwanted pregnancy and the emotional, mental health issues associated with all of these, are not considered desirable by any sector of the population.

In Britain we have little experience of health interventions other than those reliant on providing information and attempting to improve services. Both of these models are adult in their perspective and many young teenagers do not find them helpful. It is apparent that no method has had more than very limited success with positive results being confined to research experiments and dissemination from these experiments has not been shown to result in effective programmes. Some will say this is due to spurious results in inadequate social experiments, others point to the difficulty in maintaining novel approaches which may be imperfectly understood when changing from research to service mode. However, imperfect as these experiments may have been it is currently true that only programmes based on theories such as social learning,[17] social inoculation[18] and social norms[19] have demonstrated behavioural change. Behind these theories is a concept that teenage behaviour is only partly related to knowledge and is more dependant on their social environment and their efficacy and skill to determine their own actions. New behaviours are best learnt by collaboration between "teachers" and learners", rather than delivered to them in didactic style. Some actions may run contrary to the prevailing pressures they feel from their own peer group and the effectiveness of a programme which aims to see changes in behaviour will depend on students developing their self-esteem and self-efficacy. Once developed and used new behaviours become self re-enforcing. Social learning theory suggests that a previous behaviour is the strongest predictor of future action even when circumstances change. Within school based sex education obviously much of the behaviour will be learnt vicariously and in role play. The impact of this artificial situation is strengthened when it is developed in a group or class which therefore begins to change the social environment. Peer educators form an essential catalyst for change working collaboratively with the students in a programme which also encourages students to be able to express opinions and concerns and to listen to those of others in the group.

Despite the assertion of Kirby *et al.* (1994)[20] that effective programmes used social learning theories as a foundation for programme development, there has, unfortunately, been widespread variation in the interpretation of these theories in interventions. This may have delayed their development, and has certainly caused difficulty in their dissemination. In reviewing research and active projects to define the theoretical perspective for the APAUSE project (described below) it became apparent that collaboration between those delivering and those receiving a programme was the most important process if interventions were to be effective.

Peer-education, despite its history, is a new technology in sex education in this country. There is a tendency to treat it as a discrete entity with a uniform theoretical perspective though this is far from the case with considerable variation in both theoretical basis and practical application. We argue that peer education should be only one component of school sex education, the remainder being delivered by a variety of adult teachers, possibly with outside experts.

Peer led education is logistically difficult and expensive in time and resources. Without clear aims it becomes simply another, albeit novel, process attracting attention by its novelty but no more likely to be effective than other more traditional sex education models. There is no one specific protocol defined for peer education. Is it the peer *per se* that is the required component, what the peer does, or both? It is clearly inefficient to try to turn peers into experts in areas where they may have no prior expertise or experience. Although peer educators have been used as counsellors, it may be impossible to give them the appropriate interpersonal skills that allow them to counsel rather than simply tell others what to do. This will even apply to areas, such as bullying or drug taking, where teenagers may be more experienced than adults. Similarly in dealing with small groups it is likely to be difficult for young teenagers, without extensive training, to develop sufficient understanding of group dynamics to let discussions develop and they may simply have to rely on their street credibility to maintain control. Indeed it is probable that some peer education relies entirely on this credibility with younger peers to allow them to appear to make wise pronouncements about how one should behave.

Peer educators may be expected to depend more on their own personal experience than a carefully structured programme for which they have been trained. It may be safe to share some experiences or at least feelings about situations but talking about oneself is not counselling, and in school sex education sharing knowledge of experience may lead to long-lasting unhappiness when that knowledge becomes common to the rest of the school. Outside school, small group or one to one peer education with older individuals may be effective when specific common skills are needed, for example, when dealing with pregnancies. In this case there may be no danger in defining the peer leader as having had a previous or current pregnancy. However, bringing older individuals, or even same age, into schools because they have had some specific experience leads to their being set apart from others and may account for the lack of effectiveness using this as a method in school sex education. Similarly this applies to those who are brought in specifically because of their lack of experience, e.g., nominated virgins who pronounce the virtues of their state.

The credibility and standing of peer educators should not be disregarded but they should be allowed to use their abilities in a collaborative manner, allowing younger teenagers to develop their own abilities to communicate and deal with relationships. To do that, peer educators need a framework for their work in school, which should not be seen as restricting the action of peer leaders but allowing them to deliver an effective programme to a wide variety of teenagers.

Implementation of a peer-led programme

Marion Howard's[21] teen services programme in Atlanta contains a peer-led component based on social learning theory. This programme has been extensively used in North America and has formed the basis for our work in this country. Based at Exeter University and funded by a research grant from The South West Regional Health Authority and Research and Development Directorate of the South and West NHS Executive, the APAUSE (Adding Power and Understanding in Sex Education) project was established in 1990. Two research workers, based at the Department of Child Health of Exeter University, one a doctor, the other a teacher, devised a programme based on theoretical constructs and a literature search. This was initiated in two schools and evaluated using local and distant controls. The results of the programme were published[22] and the project now operates in eight local high schools, serving nearly 7,000 young people aged 12–16.

Increasingly close collaboration with local schools and the communities which they serve is sought and the project now offers:

- *Curriculum support materials for Year 7 or 8 (aged 11–13 years);*
- *Three, one hour sessions led by visiting teachers and school nurses to Year 9 (aged 13–14 years) pupils;*
- *Four sessions led by 'peer leaders' (recruited from VIth forms & College of Further Education);*
- *A further four sessions in Year 10 (aged 14–15 years) and,*
- *An annual report to each institution. This serves both as an evaluation of the project and audit of the Personal, Social and Health Education curriculum, based on a confidential questionnaire completed by pupils in Year 11 (mean age 16).*

Now funded by the North and East Devon Health Authority, in Devon, the project continues to use distant controls in comparable areas to validate the work. The project is also operating as a service provision in two other areas and is funded locally by North Essex Health and North Teesside Health Authority.

The results of the programme were, we believe, unique in Europe and rely on a collaborative process between Education and Health professionals supported by young people themselves. The results consistently demonstrate that pupils, aged 16, receiving the programme:

- *Increased their knowledge about sex, contraception and STD's;*
- *Were less likely to believe that intercourse is important in relationships;*
- *Were more tolerant of the behaviour of others and were*
- *Less likely to be sexually active.*

They were also nearly twice as likely to say sex education was 'OK', compared to the control groups! The data from our 1997 questionnaire shows comparable results. This suggests replicability to different institutions with newly trained staff and, more significantly, from research to service mode.

The project does not rely entirely on either concerned adults or well-meaning youngsters but draws on a rigorous theoretical framework and best practice from around the world. Working together, adults and young people can capitalise on the advantages that sensitive experienced professionals can offer, augmenting this with the enthusiasm and realism of youth, working for the best interests of the young people — the future — of our communities.

Howard's American classroom activities needed significant revision for use in Britain. There are cultural and teaching differences. In many ways her classes appeared to be formal in organisation but the peer leaders were extremely extrovert and the younger teenagers responded to a "show business" approach. In APAUSE we have devised four sessions led by peer educators which revolve around distinct activities. It should be noted that these sessions comprise 40% of what is otherwise an adult led intervention. The peer-led sessions involve presentation, group work, and role plays. It is a collaborative approach, peer-leaders do not instruct younger teenagers how to behave nor impose their own experiences or values onto the younger students. The sessions are not however, free from value judgements because discussion will include values that the younger students consider important. For example, students are asked, in groups, to write down all the reasons young teenagers (aged 13/14 years) might have for having sexual intercourse in a relationship and reasons why they might not. They are then asked to discuss which of the factors they consider are reasons they would approve of for themselves or for a friend. Universally, and perhaps unexpectedly, younger teenagers denigrate and reject reasons related to undue pressure or reasons that include promoting the image of one partner at the expense of another. These are the majority of reasons which they consider are behind most sexual activity at their age. It is therefore possibly not surprising that when peer-leaders discuss physical expressions of affection the vast majority of 13/14 year olds believe that people of their age should stop short of sexual intercourse in their relationships. The only surprised individuals may be adults who believe that this would not be the case.

This may be a distinct problem for adults teaching sex education since although the teenagers may not consider that sex is a current part of adult life, they will believe that the adult has at least had intercourse at some time! This may imply that sexual intercourse is an expected outcome of sex education. Teenagers may be unwilling to feel outdone by a sexually experienced adult and over-express their wishes and desires for physical activity in relationships. Because peer educators do not discuss their own experiences, neither during selection nor delivery of the sessions, the discussions do not take on the competitive atmosphere that may occur in some adult-led sex education.

Peer-led sessions do not need to include every aspect of human sexuality. Indeed it is efficient to attempt to make peer leaders into experts about contraception or STD's. This has been tried in some programmes and been criticised for attempting to make peer educators into adult presenters. If teenagers are asked to devise their own content, or make suggestions regarding the content they believe should be delivered to younger students, they frequently restrict themselves to the more biological aspects of sexual activity. This may, in part, relate to expectations they feel that adults have, particularly those involved in the programme. Peer leaders may also be identifying their own gaps in knowledge, rather than allowing themselves to recognise their strengths in talking about teenage relationships.

Peer educators are much more able to discuss and acknowledge that it is reasonable to worry and be concerned about pregnancy and STD's. Allowing open discussion about such concerns at least surmounts the barriers of denial or exaggeration, which may be a major factor in preventing young teenagers protecting themselves against pregnancy and disease. They can also discuss the problems faced when trying to access health services or even buying condoms. When dealing with the details of STD's or the effectiveness of contraceptive methods it may be more efficient and effective to use adults who have a professional training in dealing with these topics. It is, of course, these adults who teenagers, or anyone else, is likely to have to deal with if they encounter problems. Teaching teenagers how to deal with adults providing health services in the teenagers own territory of the classroom may also be an effective process in overcoming some of the power imbalance felt by those using health services.

A programme based on relationships with definite classroom activities can be delivered to whole school classes in normal curriculum time. This is a distinct advantage in sustaining the intervention. Some peer-led programmes have had early success in implementation but if it this necessitates disruption of the timetable then the programme frequently withers. The problem faced with any curriculum is to prevent the delivery becoming stale, obviously a problem for anyone teaching the same topic for some years. This is circumvented in long term peer-led education by recruiting new leaders thereby restricting the service requirement of any individual. Although this reduces the problems associated with constant repetition it increases the need for frequent training. This may also perpetuate a naiveté of delivery and apparently reduce the overall competence of the peer educators' team. In some respects this is an advantage since the younger teenagers in the class, starting their own relationships, may well identify with a naive and sometimes timid approach. To adult observers the lack of some professional skills may cause concern. Peer educators starting out to deliver sessions may be tied to their session notes and the lessons appear 'scripted'. Interestingly the pupils do not appear to be similarly concerned and whereas they would probably rebel if adults delivered in the same manner, they do not complain when it is someone more like themselves leading the sessions. It is possible to balance both aspects by retaining some members of the team for more sessions, perhaps spanning two or three years. As these peer educators become more experienced they are able to take on a training role. If, at times, they are less active in the sessions, newer team members can grow in confidence.

Negotiations with schools

Despite the increasing centralisation of the curriculum, schools remain diverse in practice, ethos and approach. As management strategies have been adopted from industry, there has been a change in the role and title of many personnel in schools. Many educationalists have been pleased to watch the traditional divide between curricular and pastoral responsibilities become more blurred. Although such changes have clarified many strategies in schools and enhanced learning opportunities, new management-speak can lend confusion to the situation. Who is the right individual (or team) to approach when developing an initiative? At least you knew both where you were and, more importantly, who you were talking to with the "Deputy Head (Pastoral)"!

Schools remain dynamic and exhilarating environments — even if many teachers would prefer to slow the velocity of this particular wind of change. As with any institution that is people-oriented, it is the personnel and the quality of the relationships between them that makes all the difference. Into the maelstrom of new initiatives that daily bombard any school, has been added peer education. Despite the minefields that surround programmes that may be described as 'student centred', involving students as an integral part of their own learning is central to many initiatives in schools today. As such, peer education is very much part of this process and has justifiably gained in popularity and in some cases, effectiveness.

There are well-documented studies which report on the benefits to the peer educators themselves.[4] Such gains are of particular interest not only to the peers themselves but to teachers responsible for these students. They recognise the advantages accrued not only to the younger students with whom the peers work, but the interest that universities or prospective employers inevitably show in students who have contributed to peer education programmes. These gains may be accredited in terms of vocational awards, improved self esteem, communication skills or simply the 'differentness' exhibited by assertive, newly empowered peer educators.

Before accepting a programme that includes peer education, schools and colleges are right to demand something more than the programme being "a good thing". One college in the authors' experience, had thought that peer education would give licence to 17 year old boys to trawl the lower years for potential partners! Clearly, teachers, parents and governors are also right to insist on evidence based evaluation prior to accepting or developing any programme. If the programme is innovative it must be soundly based in accepted theory and carefully evaluated to ensure good, improving practice.

However sound the theory or evident the benefits to the peer educators and the pupils, schools will differ in their preparedness to accept an outside intervention. Principally this is dictated by the culture of the institution which directly stems from the personnel involved. Institutional organisation and the ease with which they can adapt the curriculum are determined largely by the personnel and their philosophy. The different ways that institutions organise themselves, from four to eight session day; one and two week timetables; setting, streaming and grouping; in modular or linear patterns and the variety of different curricular models into which an initiative may be dovetailed, demand individual attention. Given the same sex education intervention, some schools have re-ordered the curriculum whilst others have found it difficult to accept components of the programme in competition with outside pressures. Such pressures inevitably include the National Curriculum, SATs, GCSEs, league tables or the usual 'quart-into-pint-pot' demands on the timetable. To compensate for this, there seems to be little substitute for frequent personal contact and regular, persistent, two-way communication.

Schools who effectively support the aims and ethos of Personal, Social and Health Education have usually been prepared to accommodate peer education. One of the challenges for both the institution and individual staff is a preparedness to relinquish their imposed control over young people. Despite lip service to the contrary, some schools and their staff are reluctant to empower the young people whose interests they exist to serve. Hiding behind control and discipline systems, reactionary cultures may deny students the opportunity to accept a real responsibility for their own learning.

Negotiation with schools needs therefore to remain on a person to person basis and be mindful of the individual needs of different institutions. If outsiders to convince an institution of the validity of either a programme of study or a methodology to implement that programme, common values need to be identified, communicated and understood. The intervention must be clear as to its overall aims, the shorter term objectives and methods of evaluating when or how each of these has been met. Why, how and when the peer educators are to work must be clearly established. The training of peer educators needs to be based both on theory and knowledge recognising the needs of the project in question. An intervention is doomed to fail however, if it is imposed irrespective of the culture of a specific institution. Collaboration is essential to establish a degree of local ownership.

Regular personal communication — preferably with the Senior Management Team and with parents and Governors must be established. Ideally, a 'steering group' is organised in each individual school to anticipate, monitor and reflect upon the reality of the programme as experienced by the school. This should include influential members of staff and representatives from the Governor and Parent bodies. More sceptical colleagues may be encouraged to express their opinions through this forum to constructively challenge the methodologies employed.

Peer recruitment

Although there are students whose actions are directed apparently for personal gain, there is a refreshing altruism in many (older) teenagers. Much has been written concerning the conflicting responsibilities regarding who decides the content of a peer-led programme. For these young people to work effectively with their peers, they need to adopt a degree of ownership of both the content and methodologies of the programme that they deliver. Some peer education projects are accused of bringing an 'adultist' agenda to their work. As discussed above, this may be an issue in projects designed to tackle substance misuse-use but of less significance in sex education. The altruistic and self-protective attitudes of young people almost inevitably lead them to recommend healthy sex choices for their (younger) peers — even if this is not directly mirrored in their own behaviour.

Schools, with unique knowledge of their students, must be involved in the selection of potential peer educators who bring their own networks and 'street cred'. These may include influential young people, who's values and lifestyles cause concern for adults. Some 'difficult' teenagers have expressed a wish to be involved in a project to help younger teenagers avoid some of the problems they have faced. It is our experience that some peer educators, who initially gave the adults cause for concern, can become some of the most effective and influential peer educators.

Younger students need to identify with their (older) peers, and respond appropriately to the objectives and methodologies of the programme. The peer educators must be 'real' in the eyes of the younger students. Clearly a group of culturally restricted educators, whether that distance be ethnic, academic or behavioural, will not be able to interact successfully the peers with whom they are working. Peer educators who are exclusively academic high flyers or "goody-two-shoes", cannot, by definition, be peers of a group which reflects the full academic and social range. Peer educators need to represent a wide range of backgrounds with which young people can identify. They do not need to be too 'slick' and will be no less effective if they occasionally stumble when speaking to the group, miss a cue or exhibit uncertainty or nervousness. The knowledge component of a peer education programme is not the most important aspect and although trainers would not encourage it, a miss-spelt word on the chalk board may not be a source of ridicule but arguably contribute to developing rapport between peer groups.

The recruitment of peer educators, therefore, needs to reflect the culture of the students with whom they will work. A common problem appears to be recruitment of male peer educators. For a range of cultural reasons, young men often require extra input before they are convinced of the value of being a peer educator. Publicity which appeals to altruism, education and social opportunity to do good, does not immediately attract all young men. Emphasising the practical and more immediate reasons for volunteering seem to attract a better response. Failing that, persistent personal invitation and, one peer educator assured us, the plethora of young female peer educators may have the desired effect! Clearly the educators need to be sympathetic to the aims, objectives and methodologies of the programme, but they also must present role-models with whom their peers can closely identify. In recruiting and training the peer educators, the facilitators must anticipate the emotions that the peer educators will experience. These include excitement, apprehensiveness, empowerment and frustration. The prospect of standing up in front of a group of their peers (albeit a couple of years younger) and leading a discussion on a sensitive issue, especially sex, touches even the strongest of hearts with trepidation. One sixteen year old female peer educator reflected: *"The thought of not knowing what they would come up with made me sweat a bit."*

Having discussed the need to evaluate the behavioural influence made by the peer educators on the students with whom they work, it is no less essential to monitor the needs and development of the peer educators. There is clear evidence of the knowledge, values, skills and self-esteem gains made by the peer educators during the course of their training and their implementation of the programme. There are considerable academic and psychological explanations for these changes. However, who could express this better than a sixteen year old male peer educator: *"Keep up the good work people, 'cos without people like you the next generation could be a bunch of ill-educated, sex mad prats!"*?

Peer training

Some peer-led initiatives have been accused of simply providing adults and, by implication, the establishment, with a teenage mouthpiece. This has been refuted above but it worth reminding the sceptics that successful recruitment of peer educators relies both on recommendation and self selection along with methodological acceptance the peer educators themselves. In the APAUSE project, peers work from a scripted text but are encouraged to change the wording to what is comfortable for them. In reviewing their training, one peer reflected that *"Getting peers to write on the scripts is very important. It is useless them telling you* (the project adults) *after a session that the script was patronising or 'cheesy'. This needs to be sorted out at the initial training."*

Presumably the students who are recommended as potential peer educators and do not participate or withdraw after an initial 'taster' session may be voicing their disquiet at the content or methodology. Conversely, our evidence suggests that the vast majority remain within the project, are happy both with the content message and are confident that they are not being manipulated.

Peer educators who are being trained to deliver a collaborative process, need to experience their training in the same model. This allows for questioning and discussion regarding content. Some peer educators have expressed the need to learn more facts: *"...so that we can tell the kids we're working with the facts."* Although the knowledge component of training (as with the sessions they facilitate) is significant, especially if peer educators are to correct "mythunderstanding", it is not the most important part of their training. The APAUSE peer educators do undergo training to familiarise themselves with the four sessions that they deliver to each class group. The peer educators are jointly trained by 'Super peer' educators from the previous year(s) and adult staff who deliver other aspects of the intervention. These are experienced teachers, including those with drama specialists and medical staff. The medics include School nurses, some with Family Planning Association training, General Practitioners and a Paediatrician. All of these staff also have personal experience of receiving the training process and leading the sessions that the peer educators deliver.

The peer educators are also trained in a variety of issues that include classroom control; drama and improvisation skills; their own sexual knowledge; the difficulties of pressure on relationships; assertiveness skills and risk appreciation. Although we regularly review the training process both from the observations of trainers and with contributions from the peer educators, preparing the peer educators for work in the classroom remains a challenging, exciting and dynamic process.

Maintaining the programme

Many peer led initiatives, ours included, are managed from outside the individual schools. The process of maintaining such a programme becomes an exercise in keeping plates spinning. Although the outside management team may remain relatively constant, the schools, their students and the peer leaders regularly change. Each year the process needs to be re-explained.

Negotiations require an annual round of discussions with schools, including those responsible for time-tabling and curriculum development. New cohorts of parents need to be informed of the background, aims and content of the programme. Annual reviews are necessary to identify strengths and weaknesses and allow full involvement in the project. This also improves the effectiveness of peer-leader identification for the forthcoming year. A set itinerary for recruitment, training, and delivery of the programme is an absolute requirement. Peer leaders are recruited well in advance and they need to know how much time they will need to devote to the programme although some will gain accreditation as part of their course work. Throughout the recruitment, training and delivery, peers will need information and reminding of the work that needs to be done. Substantial management and secretarial backup are necessary for successful maintenance over several years.

The logistics of peer-led education are probably as complex as the actual classroom work. Peers need to know who they inform if unable to attend sessions, and peer managers often end up spending several hours on the telephone to maintain their teams throughout the school year. They may need transport from colleges to schools and peer managers have spent anxious moments on street corners waiting for their teams to turn up. Added anxiety is caused by the strange glances attracted from passers-by as young teenagers pile into your car and are hurriedly driven off — not forgetting that those involved in transportation require adequate insurance cover. When the programme is finished for individual peers they are likely to need records of achievement or references from the project which also demands an efficient framework of support.

Evaluation

Increasingly, activity in schools is subject to some form of evaluation and there are considerable pressures on schools to justify any additions to a crowded curriculum. Evaluation adds to the logistic problems of implementing any school based programme although both outcome measures and quality control are both possible to measure. Direct measures of skills and knowledge gained can be made. Correct information about social norms, for example knowledge of the low prevalence of sexual activity amongst young teenagers, are easily measured and successful peer education should see major changes in this parameter. Group, individual work and role-plays lead to written documentation. Collated, these provide comparative and anonymous data that allows some standardisation of programme delivery but also provides information about programme development. Peer educators discussing the results from such evaluation will often be able to suggest ways to improve sessions and to improve the way they work. New ideas and attitudes will also come from the class students.

The process of data collection is increasingly well understood by school staff and enlisting the help of teachers to supervise questionnaires, considerably enhances data collection. This process also forces those implementing the programme to have clear aims and objectives.

In the past it may have been considered sufficient to assess a programme on the basis of student involvement, acceptability and the professional judgement of the class teacher. Given the high costs and expectations of funding agents, evaluation of peer education now needs to supply more information about potential health benefit. Although individual components of any health education may not have direct influence on individual or population health, it is still possible to identify proxy measures that will determine whether a programme is likely to compliment other work.

Additional information from research or service programme that have resulted in health benefit, allows comparative quality control measures to be made. Some measures are based in the theoretical model used to derive the programme content, others may relate to knowledge gains. This does not imply that previous measures of acceptability may not also be included. In a collaborative programme it remains extremely important that students consider the work to be of value to themselves. If absentee rates decrease during the peer sessions, or any other component of sex education, this implies a welcomed programme. Other explanations can be deduced from attendance, for example if not all the teaching staff are in full support they may remove students from sessions for activities that are considered more important. Those observing lessons should also be canvassed for their opinions about the class and their reaction to the sessions. These opinions are particularly important in assessing and maintaining school support for the programme.

Finally, assessment about health-related behaviour should be a major part of the evaluation. This may be a long term measure, not necessarily evaluated in the same year as the peer programme. It may be difficult to ascribe long term behavioural changes solely to peer-led education.

The peer-led component of the **APAUSE** programme is regularly monitored and evaluated. The knowledge, skills and attitudes of the peers are measured through quantitative questionnaires and more qualitative focus and interview sessions. The knowledge gain and changes in attitude of the school pupils are measured by 'pre' and 'post' intervention anonymised questionnaires. The programme is also evaluated through an annual questionnaire now administered to over 4,000 Year 11 (mean age 16) students. To further evaluate the effectiveness of the peers, we have also led similar sessions using the adult teaching and medical personnel instead of the 16–17 year olds. The initial results are of considerable interest and we would reasonably hope to publish in 1997.

Milburn[23] notes the dearth of well-evaluated projects in the UK, frequently with "*an inadequately specified theoretical base.*" and research is needed to determine which components of sex education might be absolute requirements. Current information suggests that peer sessions do produce major shifts in social beliefs and expectations about relationships. Correlating all of these measures at least ensures that peer-led education is part of a programme which is appreciated and effective in achieving both short and long term goals.

Project dissemination

Many peer-led projects have been established and some may continue for relatively long periods of time. Despite a wealth of knowledge gained from these projects many disappear, partly due to lack of funding and perhaps because of the logistic difficulties. Schools are used to uniformity in their work and have well-designed curricula either developed by themselves or nationally imposed. It is probably surprising to schools that health should fund so many individual and non-standard interventions. These may attract substantial investment in their early stages of investigation but are not supported in the long term even if they are shown to be effective. Problems do arise in the transformation from research to service mode. Some projects may only be effective when they have the interest and personal supervision by highly motivated research workers. These projects may too complex and require too much support to form the basis of widespread constant components of a school's sex education programme. Peer education is particularly likely to suffer from its complexity.

Conclusion

There are probably two main conclusions to be drawn working in the domain of peer education. The first is that if properly implemented, a peer education programme has the potential to offer a methodology and outcomes that differ significantly from those which can be achieved through more traditional approaches.

The second is that this potential can only be realised and, will only be understood and used to best effect, if more research is undertaken.

As the APAUSE programme in Exeter has moved from research to service mode we have established a successful protocol to recruit, train and maintain a peer-led sex education programme in 8 comprehensive schools using more than 80 peer educators. Three of the eight have their own VIth forms on site, the others rely on students who are effectively visitors to each school as the are recruited from a College of Further Education.

Although the logistics of this continue to present challenges, we are establishing evidence to suggest that not only are the peer

educators effective in their own right but that they may well be
more effective than adults leading the same sessions. This leads us
to support the accepted wisdom that effective sex education probably needs a collaborative approach but that it also needs both
adult-led *and* peer-led components. Such a programme, although
not cheap, remains beyond the financial capabilities of individual
schools and Local Education Authorities. The APAUSE programme, funded as it is to support the equivalent of one full-time
Teacher and one full-time Nurse may appear expensive. However, it has to be recognised that many Health Authorities through
agencies such as the School Nurse and Health Promotion Units
have staffing equivalents up to, and beyond, this level.

Precise financial costs of teenage termination of pregnancy and
treatment of STD's may be reasonably estimated. However, the
treatment costs for those find themselves infertile, as a result of
STD's (e.g. Chlamydia) when they do want to start families, is
more difficult to ascertain. Equally, although some of the financial costs of unwanted teenage sexual activity may be guessed at,
there are costs beyond measure of the social, emotional and men
tal health trauma suffered by boys and girls who are unable to
resist the unwelcome pressure of others.

As a society we are faced with stark choices concerning the health
and well-being of future generations. Should we continue to (under) fund projects which lack a theoretical basis, academic credibility and either do not measure or show little effect in terms of
measurable behavioural outcomes? We argue that investment
needs to be made to support programmes based on the best available theory and practice, to produce significant results. None of
these programmes are "cut and dried" but are surely worthy of
sustained research investment. Can we afford to do otherwise?
We may not be able to the change the opinions of society's adults
which parallel those concerns expressed in China so long ago, but
at least we may be able to move some way towards it!

References

1. Department of Health (1992), *The Health of the Nation: a strategy for Health in England.* London: HMSO.

2. Johnson, A.M., Wadsworth, J., Wellings, K. and Field (1994), Sexual Attitudes and Lifestyles *Blackwell Scientific Publications.*

3. Mellanby, A.R., Phelps, F. and Tripp, J.H. (1995), Added Power and Understanding Sex Education – The Project and Results. University of Exeter.

4. Allen, A.L. (1976), Children as Teachers, London: Academic Press.

5. Klepp, K.I., Halpera and Perry, C. L. (1986), The Efficacy of Peer Leaders in Drug Abuse Prevention. *Journal of School Health* 56(9): 407–411.

6. Perry, C.L. (1987), Results of prevention programmes with adolescents. *Drug and Alcohol Dependence* 20: 13–19.

7. Glynn, T.J. (1989), Essential Elements of School Based Smoking Prevention Programmes. *Journal of School Health* 59(5): 181–188.

8. Rees J.B. and Mulligan A.M. (1996), "A Peer-led scheme to ease the transition from Primary to Secondary School." 1996 (Unpublished).

9. Carr, R. Editorial (April 1996) *Peer Counselling Journal.*

10. Sciacca, J.P. (1987), Student Peer Health Education: A Powerful yet Inexpensive Helping Strategy. *The Peer Facilitator Quarterly* No.5.

11. Jacquet, S., Robertson, N. and Dear, C. (1996), The Crunch *Fast forward Positive Lifestyle Ltd.*

12. Topping, K. (1988), "The Peer Tutoring Handbook" (page 4) Croom Helm, New York.

13. Kirby, D. (1989), Research on effectiveness of sex education programmes. *Theory into Practice*: 28(3): 165–71 (Ohio State University, USA).

14. Fong, S. (1994), Youth to youth Sexual Health Education Programmes: Summary Report *Toronto Department of Public Health.*

15. Regis, D. (1996), Peer tutoring seems to work – but why? *Education and Health* 13(5): 75–78 Exeter University.

16. Kolbe, L. (1981), Propositions for an alternative and complimentary health education paradigm *Health Education* May–June, 24–30.

17. Bandura, A. (1976), Social Learning Theory, Prentice – Hall Inc., Englewood Cliffs.

18. McGuire, W.J. (1964), Advances in Experimental Social Psychology 1:83.

19. Baric, L. and Harrison, A. (1977), Social Pressure and Health Education. *The Journal of the Institute of Health Education*. 15:4;12–18.

20. Kirby, D., Short, L., Collins, J., Rugg, D., Kolbe, L., Howard, M., Miller, B., Sonestein, F. and Zabin, L.S (1994), "School-Based Programmes to Reduce Sexual Risk Behaviours: A review of effectiveness." *Public Health Reports* 109(3).

21. Howard, M. and McCabe, J.B. (1990), Helping teenagers postpone sexual involvement *Family Planning Perspectives* 22(1): 21–26.

22. Mellanby, A.R. (1995), A sex education programme with medical and educational benefit *British Medical Journal* Vol. 311. 477–453.

23. Milburn, K. (1995), A Critical Review of Peer Education with Young People with Special Reference to Sexual Health. *Health Education Research* 19(4): 407–420.

NINE

Developing Lesbian and Gay Identity in Adolescence

Adrian Coyle

Introduction

For young people who are sexually attracted to those of the same sex as themselves, the teenage years can be an immensely difficult time as they try to make sense of these attractions and incorporate them into their ideas about themselves. This chapter focuses on the tasks involved in developing a sexual identity in adolescence, i.e., the issues that many young people have to confront with the development of their thoughts and feelings about their sexuality and about themselves. It examines the potential risks that this process might create for the psychological well-being of lesbian and gay young people and considers how those who work with young people might help reduce these risks.

To counter the risk of pathologising lesbian and gay sexual identities, it is important to state that although this chapter focuses on potential problems in developing a lesbian or gay identity, many lesbian and gay young people cope resourcefully with the difficulties of creating a workable and satisfying sexual identity. Also, it may be the case that those who encounter the most serious mental health problems when struggling with a lesbian or gay identity do so because of childhood experiences that have already left them psychologically vulnerable. Although dealing with a lesbian or gay sexual identity may not be the fundamental cause of psychological difficulties in these cases, the demands of this process may transform a vulnerability into an actual mental health problem. Therefore such demands must be acknowledged, discussed and analysed if effective services are to be developed to reduce the likelihood of mental health problems arising among lesbian and gay young people and to promote effective coping among those who experience problems.

Defining terms: Lesbian, gay and bisexual

Before considering the development of lesbian and gay identity in adolescence, it is worth defining some of the key terms that will be used in this chapter. The terms "lesbian" and "gay" will be used rather than "homosexual" because these are seen as carrying more positive evaluations of same-sex feelings, behaviours and identities and because they are not focused solely on sexual issues. "Lesbian" and "gay" are terms used to describe sexual and emotional feelings and behaviours which an individual experiences towards a person of the same sex as themselves, with "lesbian" referring to the feelings and behaviours of women-oriented women and "gay" referring to the feelings and behaviours of men-oriented men.

As well as being applied to feelings and behaviours, these terms are often applied to *people* whose sexual and emotional feelings and behaviours are exclusively or predominantly directed towards others of the same sex. If someone identifies themselves as lesbian or gay, this may give a sense of certainty, stability and security to their sexual identity. However, sexual identity may not be stable over time. Research suggests that the extent to which an individual is attracted to men or women may change, sometimes radically. This has been interpreted in different ways. Some writers say that a person's fundamental sexual orientation, i.e., the extent to which they are attracted to men or women, does not change. Instead, what changes is their ability to accept their sexual orientation, act upon it, define themselves in terms of it and make it a public part of their identity. However, other writers maintain that sexual orientation is changeable, shifting and fluid and so care is needed when applying the terms "lesbian" and "gay" to people.

Of course, the terms "lesbian", "gay" and "heterosexual" (which refers to sexual and emotional feelings and behaviours experienced towards a person of a different sex) do not cover all the ways in which sexual feelings and behaviours may be experienced and expressed. It has long been recognised that people's sexual feelings and behaviours are not always exclusively oriented towards others of the same or a different sex. Some people's sexual feelings and/ or behaviours are directed towards both men and women, although not always to the same extent. These people may identify themselves as "bisexual".

However, there is no necessary connection between the nature of an individual's sexual feelings and their sexual behaviours. A woman who is sexually attracted to other women may not have sexual relations with women but may instead become sexually involved with men, perhaps because of social pressures. In the same way, there is no necessary connection between a person's sexual feelings and behaviours and their sexual identity. A man may be sexually attracted to other men and may have sex with other men but may still identify himself as heterosexual. This is possible if he defines his sexual activities with men as "just mucking around" or as "not real sex", so that these activities do not affect how he thinks of himself. Also, a woman may identify herself as lesbian but may occasionally engage in sexual relations with men: she may choose to retain a lesbian identity for political reasons or because she defines lesbian identity as being predominantly but not exclusively women-focused. It is important to remember that people often respond to issues of sexual feelings, behaviours and identities in ways that are creative and not easily predictable (see the chapters by Power and Eadie in Simpson's[1] questioning book on lesbian and gay identity).

The development of lesbian and gay identity

Many writers and researchers have offered descriptions of the experience of developing a lesbian or gay identity. Some have organised this process into stages, with individuals seen as passing through a certain number of stages *en route* to the establishment of a lesbian or gay identity. However, stage models are fraught with problems and have attracted much criticism. For example, some stage models imply that individuals progress through stages in a particular order. Although some young people may experience all the stages in a model in the specified order, others may experience only some of the stages and others may experience stages of development that have not been included within the model.

Readers who wish to find out more about stage models of lesbian and gay identity development are referred to Davies'[2] review of three well-known models. In the present chapter, the development of lesbian and gay identity is more flexibly considered as a set of tasks and issues that the young person encounters and addresses. Before considering some of these tasks and issues, it is necessary to examine the social context in which the development of lesbian and gay identity takes place. The nature of these tasks and issues is shaped by the attitudes towards homosexuality held by society in general and by the friends and family of a young person who is developing a lesbian or gay identity.

Social attitudes towards homosexuality

Research has indicated that, even today, social attitudes towards homosexuality are generally negative, with lesbians and gay men being seen as abnormal, unnatural, perverted, sinful, mentally ill and maladjusted.[3] These negative attitudes have been shaped by powerful social institutions such as religion and medicine (in the form of psychiatry). For example, the Judaeo-Christian tradition's condemnation of male homosexuality is based on Biblical injunctions against sexual relations between men (which are described as an "abomination"). Psychiatry — and particularly psychoanalysis —has long represented homosexuality as a form of mental illness. Although homosexuality was removed from the American Psychiatric Association's list of mental disorders in 1973, the associations of sickness and pathology continue to have negative effects on public attitudes. These associations resurfaced with the advent of AIDS, which linked gay men with disease and death in a very concrete way.

Unless they are surrounded by people who actively reject these negative views, young people who experience sexual and emotional attractions towards others of the same sex and who suspect they may be lesbian or gay are thus faced with highly negative social messages about their feelings. This may be particularly the case if their family and friends are religious or belong to a fundamentalist denomination, are politically conservative, have very traditional ideas about how men and women ought to behave or have little or no contact with lesbians or gay men. Research has indicated that these factors are particularly associated with the holding of negative attitudes towards lesbians and gay men.[4] Young people who are exploring their sexual identity in such contexts may therefore feel very negatively about their sexual feelings. They may make strenuous efforts to deny them so that they do not have to think of their feelings and themselves as lesbian or gay because to do so would pose a massive threat to their self-esteem.

Developing awareness of same-sex sexuality

Many descriptions of lesbian and gay identity development start at the point where the young person develops an awareness that their sexuality is focused on others of the same sex as themselves. They may then begin to suspect that the labels "lesbian" or "gay" could apply to their sexuality and to themselves. This process is said to spring from reflections upon their sexual thoughts, feelings and/or behaviours.

In her description of the process, Cass[5] links such awareness with feelings of confusion and turmoil. Confusion is said to arise if the young person's awareness conflicts with how they previously viewed themselves, i.e., as heterosexual or simply as "not lesbian or gay". Turmoil may result from the prospect of seeing themselves in terms of a negatively valued social category of which their friends and family may have voiced disapproval. Other researchers and writers have identified additional or related states and emotions which can accompany a young person's suspicions that they might be lesbian or gay. These include fears of hurting one's parents, not being accepted and becoming isolated, diminished self-esteem and feelings of depression, guilt, repulsion, self-hatred and frustration.

Cass[5] maintains that as the young person's suspicions about their sexuality may be quite vague at this stage, outside help is rarely sought. Instead, they may try to find out more about being lesbian or gay in an attempt to confirm or disconfirm their suspicions. However, if they find the possibility of being lesbian or gay unacceptable, the young person may deny that a lesbian or gay interpretation can be placed upon their thoughts, feelings and/or behaviours. These may instead be seen as indicating a "passing phase" of being interested in or experimenting sexually with others of the same sex. Debates in the UK parliament and in the media concerning a proposal to lower the age of consent for gay men in 1994 revealed that the idea of a "homosexual phase" is a common feature of talk about adolescent sexual development. If they previously engaged in same sex sexual activity, the young person may interpret this as simple experimentation or may deny that it ever happened. They may adopt a strong anti-lesbian and gay stance in an effort to distance themselves from the possibility that they might be lesbian or gay. These efforts can be difficult to maintain. Even if the young person manages to engage in heterosexual behaviour and avoid situations which might threaten a heterosexual identity, sexual attractions and erotic dreams focused on others of the same sex are more difficult to control.

Concerning the age at which young people start suspecting that they might be lesbian or gay, a number of writers and researchers have suggested that a sense of being different emerges in childhood (before the age of 13). As a result of sexual and/or emotional experiences, this is said to crystallise into a sense of sexual difference in adolescence (before the age of 17) which develops into a specific awareness that one might be lesbian or gay. However, this process can also evolve later in life.

Self-definition as lesbian or gay

As the individual gradually lets go of ideas of themselves as heterosexual, they risk casting themselves adrift on a sea of uncertainty. The expectations of life that most of us internalise from our parents and from the world around us presume that we will grow up, get married and have children. For lesbian and gay young people, it becomes clear that their sexual thoughts, feelings and/or behaviours do not fit with these expectations. It can be very difficult for them to construct an alternative blueprint for life if they do not have the raw materials to do so. For this reason, some young people may not define themselves as lesbian or gay until they have met other lesbians and gay men and have gained access to ideas about possible life courses that may be open to them. The average age at which self-definition as lesbian or gay is said to occur varies across studies but is generally in the 17–21 range

Initial contact with other lesbians or gay men may not, however, result in positive outcomes. This can happen if initial contact is made in a purely sexual context where there is no opportunity for social interaction, if the young person lacks the social skills needed to engage with others or if they feel that they have little in common with those whom they meet. Lesbian and gay communities — like any other communities — are not utopian, wholly welcoming and accepting places, although this is seldom acknowledged in writing on lesbian and gay identity. Negative experiences with other lesbians or gay men can result in the young person experiencing an acute sense of isolation, self-hatred and psychological strain.

On the other hand, if initial or subsequent contacts with other lesbians and gay men are validating and supportive, the young person can develop a positive sense of what it means to be lesbian or gay (as negative social messages about lesbians and gay men are counteracted) and they may become more committed to a lesbian or gay identity. Through continued social involvement with other lesbians and gay men, the young person can obtain insights into the possible courses that their life might take, allowing them to conceptualise a future for themselves as lesbian or gay. They can also learn how to cope with the interpersonal problems that being lesbian or gay can cause. In general terms, they can avail of the mutual help system that exists within many lesbian and gay communities and can obtain social support for the development of their sexual identity.

It is worth noting that when an individual defines themselves as lesbian or gay, this does not mean that they will not redefine themselves at a later stage. Changing circumstances may lead someone to set aside a lesbian or gay identity. For example, a young woman may have defined herself as lesbian and developed a positive view of being lesbian. However, if she then encounters a negative life event related to her sexual identity (such as the breakdown of a relationship or a hostile response from others to her sexual identity), this can lead her to evaluate her lesbianism negatively and to question whether she really is lesbian. The process of self-definition and developing a positive evaluation of lesbian identity may thus begin again. Alternatively, changes in the nature of a person's sexual desires or dissatisfaction with the perceived limitations of lesbian and gay identity (see Simpson[1]) may lead the individual to redefine their sexual identity.

Passing as heterosexual

According to Cass,[5] a central task which tends to arise early in lesbian and gay identity development involves handling the feeling of not belonging, of being different from family members and peers and dealing with the recognition that others may view the tentative lesbian or gay identity negatively. Feelings of isolation can be particularly acute at this point. Some individuals respond by devaluing the importance of other people's opinions of them but at the same time presenting themselves to others as heterosexual (or as not having any sexual interests) to avoid encountering negative reactions. This process whereby a person disguises the fact that they are lesbian or gay is referred to as "passing". For lesbian and gay young people, growing up has been described as a process of "learning to hide".

However, even years after having initially constructed a lesbian or gay identity, many lesbians and gay men still hide their sexual identity from at least some others in their social world, most commonly from family members, work colleagues and some friends. For example, while under a quarter of the 930 gay men studied by Davies *et al.*[6] had disclosed their sexual identity to all their family, friends and workmates, just under a third had disclosed to fewer than half of these people. This can lead to feelings of guilt, dishonesty, estrangement from others and from the self and fear of discovery. For example, when asked to describe how they felt when passing, many of the gay men studied by Coyle[7] said they felt that those from whom they disguised their homosexuality did not really know them and they wished they had the courage to tell them. They felt they were not being true to themselves, that they were "letting the side down" and being hypocritical.

While these feelings may also be associated with passing in the early stages of developing a lesbian or gay identity, passing can also allow the young person time to get used to the idea of themselves as lesbian or gay before taking that identity into the public domain. It has also been contended that passing may not be as psychologically demanding as is sometimes assumed. Over time, passing may become a routine way for an individual to deal with parts of their social world where the disclosure of sexual identity would be risky.

For lesbian and gay young people, the social implications of not always managing to pass as heterosexual can be severe. In his research, Rivers[8] described lesbians' and gay men's experiences of being bullied at school on account of their sexual identity. The most common forms of bullying they had experienced were name-calling, being subject to ridicule, being hit or kicked and being the subject of rumour or gossip. For example, one woman reported:

My desk was turned out. Photographs of naked women were thrown at me along with verbal abuse. My bag was slashed with a knife. Graffiti was written about me.

A gay man described how, as an adolescent, he had been bullied by a group of boys who burnt him with cigarettes. Some respondents said that this bullying sometimes took place in front of teachers who did nothing to intervene. Twenty of Rivers' 44 respondents told a parent about being bullied but only seven told them why they were being bullied. Likewise, although 10 told a teacher, only four also gave the reason for the bullying. Only very rarely did this alleviate the situation. Some respondents indicated that their experiences had had a longlasting negative effect on their psychological well-being, with one man saying it had left "deep psychological scars".

Disclosing lesbian or gay identity

The most obvious way of relieving the stresses of passing is to disclose sexual identity to others. Additional reasons for wanting to disclose sexual identity include a desire to put social relationships on a more honest footing and to share an important aspect of the self with others. It is vital that initial disclosures of lesbian or gay identity are handled carefully. If the young person experiences a series of negative reactions from significant others, this can reinforce negative social messages that have been internalised about being lesbian or gay and this may halt the development of sexual identity. Positive reactions, on the other hand, can facilitate the development of a positively-evaluated, psychologically satisfying lesbian or gay identity and may foster commitment to that identity.

The process of disclosing sexual identity is usually very selective, at least at first, with the person usually choosing to disclose to others whom they reckon will not react badly. For the gay men in Coyle's[7] study, the first people whom they told about their sexual identity were mostly male and female friends. Relatively few men chose to tell family members first. This may have been because negative reactions from family members could have had a highly detrimental effect on psychological well-being due to the close or dependent nature of these relationships.

Disclosure can be handled in various ways, with the most common strategy being explicit verbal disclosure. Other possible strategies identified in research include implicit verbal approaches (such as dropping hints), explicit non-verbal approaches (such as showing physical affection for a same-sex partner) and implicit non-verbal approaches (such as associating with known lesbians and gay men). The way in which disclosure is handled tends to vary with experience, with the process becoming more spontaneous and easier as more people are told. However, the anxiety associated with disclosure is most closely related to the importance of the disclosure audience. So, for example, if someone is close to their parents, the prospect of disclosing sexual identity to them may be anxiety-provoking, regardless of how often the person has disclosed to others in the past.

In Coyle's[7] study, those who were told generally reacted in either a positive or a neutral way. The most common responses were for the other person to say that it made no difference to how they felt about the individual; that they had already guessed anyway; and to ask them more about it. Very few people became upset or abusive. Given these reactions, it is not surprising that initial disclosures of sexual identity were said to have had quite positive consequences for the men involved. When asked how they felt after these disclosures, the most popular answers were that they felt relieved; they felt more comfortable about being gay; and they felt more confident. As with disclosure strategies, reactions to disclosure can change over time. With opportunities for reflection, initial negative reactions may give way to more positive or at least neutral responses.

Negative reactions to the disclosure of lesbian or gay identity may be influenced by many different factors. The person who has been told may to some extent hold the sort of negative social attitudes towards homosexuality that were outlined earlier and so may now view the discloser as abnormal, sick, perverse, sinful, etc. They may experience conflict if the discloser's sexual identity clashes with attitudes that are central to their own identity, e.g., if they hold strong religious beliefs which represent lesbian and gay sexualities as sinful. Alternatively, even if they do not hold such attitudes, the disclosure may have radically altered both their view of the discloser and the basis of their relationship, which can result in feelings of confusion and turmoil. They may feel that their previous interactions with the discloser were based on false premises and that their relationship has been invalidated. In addition, parents may react negatively to disclosure if they hold themselves responsible for their son or daughter's homosexuality and so feel guilty; if their expectations of their child were focused on their marrying and providing grandchildren; or because they fear that their child will never achieve social acceptance and will have a difficult, unhappy life.

Disclosure is not an all-or-nothing event. While lesbian and gay young people may tell some people about their sexual identity and may make concerted efforts to hide their sexual identity from others, there is a third possibility that needs to be considered. Some people in the young person's social world may not be told explicitly but the young person may not make strenuous efforts to conceal their sexual identity from them. This group usually consists of people whom the young person wishes to know about their sexual identity but whom they feel unable to tell because of the possible implications, e.g., parents and other family members.

One potentially problematic variation of the disclosure scenario arises when disclosure is not initiated by the lesbian or gay young person but by someone else. This can occur by accident (for example, when one person presumes that another already knows about an individual's sexual identity) or it can be malicious. This situation is potentially difficult because the lesbian or gay young person does not have control over the timing or content of the disclosure and may not be adequately prepared to deal with the issue if the person to whom the disclosure was made then confronts them about it.

Lesbian and gay relationships

The development of sexual and emotional relationships with other lesbians or gay men represents a major milestone in the development of lesbian and gay identity. After having struggled to think of themselves in a positive way, lesbian and gay young people may experience their first relationships as tremendously validating, suggesting to them that they deserve to give and receive love. Identity development may continue and identity commitment may increase within the context of a supportive close relationship.

Negative relationship experiences can, however, have a detrimental effect upon identity development. Initial lesbian and gay relationships may collapse under a burden of excessive expectations. Sometimes one or both partners may see the relationship as a major end point or goal of lesbian and gay identity development. They may feel that the relationship should be of sufficient quality to compensate for the struggle involved in constructing a lesbian or gay identity or to make this struggle worthwhile. They may expect that the relationship will provide a limitless supply of support, validation and security to compensate for any deficiencies that they have experienced in these domains. Also, if young lesbians and gay men have avoided close relationships with others during the development of sexual identity (perhaps because they feared their sexual identity would be discovered), they may lack the skills needed to maintain relationships. Furthermore, while heterosexual relationships — especially marital relationships — have social, religious and legal approval, lesbian and gay relationships are not officially sanctioned and so may be deprived of social support. Many lesbian and gay relationships are socially invisible to family members, colleagues and at least some friends. When family members *are* told of the relationship, they often refuse to accept it and may fail to acknowledge the significance of important milestones in the couple's joint life, such as anniversaries. Any of these factors — singly or in combination — can make initial lesbian and gay relationships vulnerable to failure. Some young people respond by adjusting their expectations of relationships and making them more realistic. The ending of relationships can lead others to a negative evaluation of what it means to be lesbian or gay or even to question their lesbian or gay identity.

For those who work with lesbian and gay young people in any sort of therapeutic context, it is important to be aware that lesbian and gay relationships differ from heterosexual relationships. The main areas of difference concern social acknowledgement and social acceptance, rates of cohabitation, the distribution of power within relationships and rules about whether or not the partners can have sex with people outside the relationship (see Kitzinger and Coyle[9] for a review of this literature). If service providers assume that the only acceptable and healthy framework for structuring relationships is that of traditional heterosexual relationships, they may try to steer lesbian and gay young people away from other relationship formats, without considering that the young person may be engaging in a form of relationship which meets their current needs. It is worth noting that there is no evidence that lesbians and gay men are any less happy with their sex lives or with their relationships than heterosexuals. Neither have any differences been found between gay men in sexually exclusive relationships and gay men in sexually open relationships in terms of relationship satisfaction or psychological adjustment.

Another reason why providers of services to lesbian and gay young people need to be aware of the differences between heterosexual relationships and lesbian and gay relationships is that young lesbians and gay men may not be aware of these differences. Having been socialised with a heterosexual blueprint for relationships, they may try to make their relationships conform to this framework. This can lead to relationship problems, especially if their partner has greater experience of lesbian and gay relationships and so has different expectations of what relationships involve. In this

case, the service provider may play an educational role in informing the young person about different relationship formats and
exploring their responses to these.

Lesbian and gay identity: A diversity of experiences

Due to differences in life circumstances and in available resources,
there is considerable diversity in the ways in which young people
address the issues and tasks associated with creating a lesbian or
gay identity. More fundamentally, the nature of the process can
be very different across different social groups. Until recently, this
was seldom acknowledged in work on lesbian and gay identity.
For example, writing and research on the topic simply assumed
that a lesbian or gay identity takes precedence over other aspects
of identity. However, people have a multiplicity of identity elements, some of which may be just as important or more important than a lesbian or gay identity. For example, Deverell and
Prout[10] found that some black gay men preferred to organise their
identity around being black rather than around being gay because
they experienced a greater need for support around issues of race.
If other identity elements conflict with a lesbian or gay identity,
the person is faced with the task of managing this conflict. For
example, Rafalin and Coyle[11] have highlighted how Jewish lesbians and gay men may experience conflict between their sexual
identity and their cultural and/or religious identity. For this group
and for others in similar positions, the task of reconciling these
identity elements adds to and complicates the process described in
most accounts of the development of lesbian or gay identity.

More generally, the particular issues faced by lesbian and gay
young people from ethnic minority communities have only begun
to be acknowledged in recent years. Although there are relatively
few positive role models for white lesbian and gay young people,
the situation is even worse for young people from ethnic minority
communities. This can contribute to the low self-esteem and
feelings of isolation experienced by many lesbian and gay young

people from ethnic minorities. Also, disclosing a lesbian or gay identity to others within an ethnic minority community may be particularly problematic if that community consists of close-knit social networks. If one person decides to tell another without the consent of the person who disclosed their sexual identity, there is a danger of information "leaking out". The lesbian or gay young person may find that they have lost control of information about their sexual identity. Those who work with young people from ethnic minority communities who are exploring sexual identity issues need to be aware of those factors which might make the development of a lesbian or gay identity different or more diffi-cult in these contexts.

Finally, it should be remembered that the development of gay male identity is different from the development of lesbian iden-tity. While some writers and researchers have produced models of the experiences of either men or women, others have focused on experiences that are common across genders. The development of gay male identity tends to be more abrupt, while the develop-ment of lesbian identity tends to be more fluid and ambiguous, perhaps because there is greater leeway for interpreting strong emotional relationships between women in non-sexual terms than in the case of strong emotional relationships between men. Due to different socialisation experiences, gay men tend to engage in sexual activity earlier and be more competitive and autonomous within their relationships (which can be a source of relationship problems), while lesbian women tend to have greater emotional attachment within their relationships.

This diversity of possible pathways through the process of cre-ating a lesbian and gay identity needs to be borne in mind because it is often omitted from writing and research on the topic. If those who work with lesbian and gay young people are mindful of this, models of lesbian and gay identity can be a valuable tool for understanding the experiences of young people who are coming to terms with a lesbian or gay identity and for planning interven-tions to promote the well-being of these young people.

Lesbian and gay young people and mental health

The research and writing that has been reviewed in this chapter suggests that when lesbian and gay young people are developing their sexual identities, they have to negotiate tasks that can potentially have adverse effects on their psychological well-being. However, research which has focused on mental health among (young) lesbians and gay men has produced mixed findings. Some studies have found that, compared with heterosexuals, lesbians and gay men have a lower level of psychological well-being. Other studies have found no difference in mental health and others have found that lesbians and gay men have a higher level of well-being. Care has to be taken when considering this research because much of it is flawed. The chief problem is that some studies have focused on atypical individuals who were already likely to have mental health problems, for example, because they were in receipt of mental health services (although, when recruiting participants for research, there is also a problem of deciding what constitutes a "typical" lesbian or gay man). One study which avoided many of these problems recruited a relatively young group of gay men through press adverts, gay groups and venues and friendship networks.[12] This research found that these men had a significantly lower level of psychological well-being than married and single men from the general population. This was attributed to

the psychological burden imposed on gay men by their having to construct a sexual identity against a backdrop of negative social representations [views] of homosexuals and homosexuality and possibly with limited support from non-gay significant others in their social world   (p. 219).

The question then arises of the extent to which this has a major negative effect upon the lives of young lesbians and gay men. Research on suicide among young lesbians and gay men suggests that the effect can be severe. This research has consistently found a markedly higher risk of suicidal thoughts and behaviours among lesbian and gay young people than among heterosexual youth. To take some specific figures from US studies, D'Augelli and Hershberger[13] found that 42 per cent of the 194 lesbian and gay young people whom they studied said they had attempted suicide. Rotheram-Borus *et al.*[14] found that 39 per cent of their young, mostly non-white, gay and bisexual male sample had attempted suicide; another 37 per cent had thought about suicide every day for at least a week at some point in their lives; and nearly 60 per cent reported suicidal ideation in the week before they took part in the study. There has been limited work on this issue in the UK, but a study conducted by Trenchard and Warren[15] with the London Gay Teenage Group found that one in five participants had attempted suicide and Bridget's[16] study of 20 relatively isolated young lesbians found that 14 had attempted suicide. Clearly, there is a problem here. From all the work conducted on this issue, Bridget[16] concluded that lesbian and gay young people are between two and six times more likely to attempt suicide than heterosexual youth.

Promoting mental health among lesbian and gay young people

Given this situation, there is a need for mental health promotion work among young people who are negotiating the process of con-structing a sexual identity. One of the major obstacles to such work is the difficulty of recruiting young lesbians and gay men to mental health promotion projects. If they are still trying to figure out whether or not they are lesbian or gay and if they are strug-gling with what being lesbian or gay might mean for them, young people may be unwilling to take part in activities that are geared specifically towards lesbians and gay men. To do so may be seen as risking a commitment to an identity that they may really only be beginning to come to terms with. Professionals who are thinking about undertaking such work with lesbian and gay young people face an uphill task in recruiting individuals to any projects they wish to establish.

If there are lesbian and gay social or political groups in the lo-cality, these can be a valuable resource. For example, one such group is Friend, an organisation with branches in many parts of the UK which provides information, advice and social activities for lesbians and gay men (see the resources section at the end of this book for the address of Friend's co-ordinating body). If such groups are not available, it may be necessary to contact individuals and organisations (such as counselling services in educational institutions and youth workers) who might act as a channel through which young people who are dealing with sexual identity issues could be referred to mental health promotion projects. Indeed, these individuals may wish to become involved in the development and facilitation of such projects.

However, not everyone is equipped to fulfil this mental health promotion role effectively. Research by Coyle and Loveless[17] has indicated that training in sexuality issues and in the development of interpersonal and communication skills may be needed to enable people to undertake such work with confidence, although previous experience will also be an asset. Davies[18] describes other qualities and skills needed to undertake any sort of therapeutic work with young people who are addressing sexual identity issues. These include respecting the young person's feelings, experiences and integrity, creating space and time for the young person to reflect upon their experiences and feelings and devising experiences which can enhance the young person's self-esteem. Let us now briefly consider how these aims might be realised.

Using groupwork

One very simple intervention involves running a series of discussion groups, focusing on specific issues related to developing a lesbian or gay identity. The potential benefits to the group participants of discussing shared concerns and exchanging shared experiences should not be underestimated. In the first place, it can be cathartic, allowing participants to express feelings that have been kept bottled up for too long. Also, discovering that others have grappled with the same problems can decrease feelings of isolation. Participants can learn strategies for dealing with problematic situations related to being lesbian or gay through listening to how others have coped with similar situations. Through all this, they can be helped to conceptualise being lesbian or gay as something positive. For those who are not involved in lesbian and gay social networks, the group could act as a springboard and preparation for such involvement. This could expose the participants to the potential social and psychological benefits that may flow from such involvement.

Some potentially difficult issues can be dealt with by using group exercises and role play. For example, group exercises can promote self-esteem among lesbian and gay young people by encouraging them to examine the negative messages about lesbians and gay men that they were exposed to when they were growing up (see Mole[19] for ideas about potential exercises). The internalisation of these messages may have led some group participants to think that any identity-related difficulties they are experiencing are due to personality problems or psychological defects. If these individuals take part in exercises which allow them to examine these messages and their effects in a critical way, they may begin to attribute any identity-related problems to the difficulty of constructing a positive lesbian or gay identity in a society that devalues that identity. This can reduce any tendency towards blaming themselves for all the problems they have encountered around being lesbian or gay.

To take an example, the group might wish to discuss issues around disclosing sexual identity. If some participants are thinking about disclosing for the first time or disclosing to someone new, the facilitator could devise group exercises that could help ensure that this has a positive outcome. A useful starting point may be to encourage the discussion or role playing of scenarios which raise general issues about the different ways in which disclosure could be approached. An example of such a scenario is presented below. This could be amended so that the main character reflects the life circumstances of the majority of group participants.

Michael is 19 years old and is a university student. After having stuggled with his sexuality since his early teenage years, six months ago he decided to do something about it. Although it took him some time to pluck up enough courage, eventually he went to a meeting of the university Lesbian and Gay Group and was warmly welcomed. For the past two months, Michael has been involved in a relationship with Andrew, a fellow student whom he met at the Group. This made him feel that it was time he told some of his friends that he was gay.

He decided to tell his friend, Fiona, whom he met during his first week at university. Since then, they have grown very close and have been able to talk about almost anything. After ensuring that his flatmates would be out for the evening, he invited Fiona around for dinner. As the evening wore on, Michael began to wonder whether he would ever find the courage to tell her and he became more and more uptight and nervous. Fiona noticed this and asked him what was wrong. He took a deep breath and, as calmly as he could, he said "I've got something to tell you. I'm gay".

This scenario could be presented to group participants who might then be asked to consider questions such as:

— How do you think Michael might feel if Fiona reacted positively/negatively to his disclosure?
— If she reacted negatively, what could he do or what should he do?
What do you think about the way he told Fiona? If you were in Michael's situation, would you have handled things differently?

The discussion that arises from these questions could lead to a sharing of actual disclosure experiences, giving participants an opportunity to learn from each other. The aims of an exercise such as this are to practise and refine strategies for disclosing sexual identity, to develop an awareness of the range of possible reactions that disclosure can elicit and to devise strategies for dealing with these reactions. After taking part in such exercises, some participants may feel confident to engage in disclosure, which could reduce the strains of passing. Others may realise that it is not yet feasible to disclose their sexual identity to certain other people in their social world, perhaps because they are particularly unsure about how these people would react and/or because they could not cope with the possible implications if they reacted very negatively. In this latter situation, discussions can be facilitated around the experience of passing, including strategies for coping with any negative feelings engendered by having to hide a lesbian or gay identity.

Counselling support for lesbian and gay young people

While it is vital to engage in work designed to promote the mental health of lesbian and gay young people and prevent major mental health problems occurring, it is equally important to ensure that high quality services are available for those who do experience such problems. When professionals encounter young people who are having particular difficulties around sexual identity issues, they are often unsure where they can refer the young person for counselling or psychotherapeutic support. This problem has been somewhat alleviated with the production of a referral list of lesbian and gay affirmative therapists by the Association for Lesbian, Gay and Bisexual Psychologies UK (whose address appears in the resources section at the end of this book). Lesbian and gay affirmative therapists are those whose practice is informed by the belief that lesbian, gay and bisexual sexualities are of equal value to heterosexuality.

Of course, the majority of these therapists work in private practice and so most young people will not have the resources to access such therapeutic support. Instead, they will have to seek therapeutic help wherever they can, for example, through school, college or GP counsellors, and hope that their counsellor or therapist does not have a negative view of lesbian and gay sexualities. If a young lesbian or gay man is being referred to therapeutic services, the person making the referral should check the service provider's attitudes to, training in and experience of lesbian and gay issues. Davies'[20] discussion of the core qualities required for affirmative practice provides useful pointers about what to look for in potentially appropriate counsellors and therapists.

The need for a proactive approach

One of the key points made in this chapter is that many of the psychological difficulties experienced by lesbian and gay young people in the identity development process stem from the internalisation of negative social messages about lesbians and gay men. Instead of trying to undo the damaging effects of these messages after they have been internalised, a more proactive approach would involve actively challenging them and making sure they are not internalised in the first place. There is little point in concentrating efforts in pulling drowning people out of the river if we do not look upstream to see who or what is pushing them in. In this case, the force pushing lesbian and gay young people into the river of lowered psychological well-being is a social context which pathologises and devalues lesbian and gay sexualities. A starting point in the effort to counteract this would be to provide children with factual and positive education on lesbian and gay sexualities in which being lesbian or gay is presented as a life choice of equal value to heterosexuality.

Yet, the provision of such education has been curtailed in the UK by popular interpretations of Section 28 of the 1988 Local Government Act. This is often seen as forbidding teaching about the acceptability of homosexuality. In fact, the prohibition is placed upon local authorities, not upon schools, and a 1994 Department for Education document[21] stated that Section 28 applies to "the activities of local authorities themselves, as distinct from the activities of the governing bodies and staff of schools on their own behalf" (p. 19).

Despite this, positive educational interventions about being lesbian or gay are contentious and arouse strong passions. For example, an excellent educational resource for schools on issues of sexuality and difference,[19] with a focus on lesbian and gay sexualities, aroused tabloid wrath when it was produced by a London NHS Trust. Nevertheless, a way must be found to provide such education because otherwise it is difficult to challenge negative social messages about homosexuality in a systematic and effective way. Without such a challenge, these messages will continue to compromise the psychological well-being of lesbian and gay young people and place their mental health at risk.

References

1. Simpson, M. (ed.) *Anti-Gay* (London: Freedom Editions, 1996), 55–83.

2. Davies, D. "Working with People Coming Out", in *Pink Therapy: A Guide for Counsellors and Therapists Working with Lesbian, Gay and Bisexual Clients*, eds. D. Davies and C. Neal (Buckingham: Open University Press, 1996), 66–85.

3. Herek, G.M. "Stigma, Prejudice, and Violence Against Lesbians and Gay Men", in *Homosexuality: Research Implications for Public Policy*, eds. J.C. Gonsiorek and J.D. Weinrich (Newbury Park, CA: Sage, 1991), 60–80.

4. Herek, G.M. "Assessing Heterosexuals' Attitudes Toward Lesbians and Gay Men: A Review of Empirical Research with the ATLG Scale", in *Lesbian and Gay Psychology: Theory, Research, and Clinical Applications*, eds. B. Greene and G.M. Herek (Thousand Oaks, CA: Sage, 1994), 206–228.

5. Cass, V.C. (1979), "Homosexual Identity Formation: A Theoreti-

cal Model" *Journal of Homosexuality* 4: 219–236.

6. Davies, P.M., Hickson, F.C.I., Weatherburn, P. and Hunt, A.J. *Sex, Gay Men and AIDS* (London: Falmer, 1993), 86.

7. Coyle, A. *The Construction of Gay Identity: Vols. 1 and 2*. Unpublished PhD thesis. University of Surrey, 1991, 413–414, 420–421, 440–441.

8. Rivers, I. (1995), "The Victimization of Gay Teenagers in Schools: Homophobia in Education" *Pastoral Care* 13: 39–45.

9. Kitzinger, C. and Coyle, A. (1995), "Lesbian and Gay Couples: Speaking of Difference" *The Psychologist* 8: 64–69.

10. Deverell, K. and Prout, A. "Sexuality, Identity and Community – Reflections on the MESMAC Project", in *AIDS: Safety, Sexuality and Risk*, eds. P. Aggleton, P. Davies, and G. Hart (London: Taylor & Francis, 1995) 172–193.

11.   Rafalin, D. and Coyle, A. "Balancing Cultural, Religious and Sexual Identity: Jewish Gay Men and Lesbians". A Workshop Presented at the *Annual Training Conference of the Association for Lesbian, Gay and Bisexual Psychologies – UK: Homophobia and Beyond*. University of Nottingham, September 13–15, 1996.

12.   Coyle, A. (1993), "A Study of Psychological Well-Being Among Gay Men Using the GHQ-30" *British Journal of Clinical Psychology* 32: 218–220.

13.   D'Augelli, A.R. and Hershberger, S.L. (1993), "Lesbian, Gay, and Bisexual Youth in Community Settings: Personal Challenges and Mental Health Problems" *American Journal of Community Psychology* 21: 421–448.

14.   Rotheram-Borus, M.J., Hunter, J. and Rosario, M. (1994), "Suicidal Behavior and Gay-Related Stress Among Gay and Bisexual Male Adolescents" *Journal of Adolescent Research* 9: 498–508.

15.   Trenchard, L. and Warren, H. *Something To Tell You...The Experiences and Needs of Young Lesbians and Gay Men in London* (London: London Gay Teenage Group, 1984).

16.   Bridget, J. "Lesbian and Gay Youth and Suicide". A Paper Presented at a Conference on *The Needs of Gay and Lesbian Young People*. National Children's Bureau, London, April 28, 1995.

17.   Coyle, A. and Loveless, L. (1995), "A Study of Youth Workers as Health Promoters on Sex-Related Issues and HIV/AIDS in a British City" *International Journal of Adolescence and Youth* 5: 157–171.

18.   Davies, D. "Working with Young People", in *Pink Therapy: A Guide for Counsellors and Therapists Working with Lesbian, Gay and Bisexual Clients*, eds. D. Davies and C. Neal (Buckingham: Open University Press, 1996), 131–148.

19.   Mole, S. *Colours of the Rainbow: Exploring Issues of Sexuality and Difference* (London: Health Promotion Service, Camden & Islington Community Health Services NHS Trust, 1995).

20.   Davies, D. "Towards a Model of Gay Affirmative Therapy", in *Pink Therapy: A Guide for Counsellors and Therapists Working with Lesbian, Gay and Bisexual Clients*, eds. D. Davies and C. Neal (Buckingham: Open University Press, 1996), 24–40.

21.   Department for Education, *Education Act 1993: Sex Education in Schools: Circular Number 5\94* (London: Department for Education, 1994), 19.

TEN

Adolescent Sexuality and Adult Professional Behaviour: Future Directions for Policy and Practice

John Coleman and Debi Roker

In this, the concluding chapter, we wish to consider some of the policy implications that flow from the contributions to this book. Adolescent sexuality poses a series of challenges for professional adults, and there is undoubtedly too little opportunity for the proper discussion and consideration of these issues, free from strident dispute and disagreement so popular with the media. Sexuality is of course a biological phenomenon, but it cannot be separated from the social dimension. Sexual behaviour occurs in social situations, and is influenced in every way by social pressures and values. It is these pressures and values we need to understand if we are to prepare young people fully and effectively for their sexual maturation.

One of the reasons that this subject is such a challenge for adults is that the social context of sexuality i.e. the values and pressures just referred to, lead to contradictions and to dilemmas which cannot easily be resolved. To end this book we wish to consider some of these dilemmas, and review the implications of what has been written here for policy in the fields of sex education, and in the provision of sexual health services for young people. These dilemmas can be framed in the form of questions, and we intend to focus on six of these which are, in our view, central to the understanding of adolescent sexuality.

1. What is the role of adults vis a vis adolescent sexuality?

This is a theme which runs through many of the chapters in this book. It is addressed by Mitchell (Chapter 6) when she asks whether adults have a responsibility to protect young people, but in addition it is implicit in almost all the contributions which explore questions to do with the nature of effective sex education. It is important to note that we are not here considering the issue of parental responsibility, although it may be that the responsibilities of professional adults have to be set in the context of the role played by the family.

It could be argued that there are four possible roles for professional adults: to protect young people from experiences which may in some way be detrimental to their development; to set boundaries and limits on their sexual behaviour; to act as advocates for young people in respect of health services and/or sex education; and lastly to provide both services and educational opportunities of the highest quality possible in the particular circumstances.

We will be referring to the latter two roles later in this chapter, and it may be that these are the least controversial. It is probably true to say that it is in relation to the first and second of these that the greatest difficulties arise. Let us look first at the problems surrounding the idea of a protective role for adults. Before we can do this we need to differentiate between professional adults. Thus for example most would probably agree that the role of politicians or legislators should include a responsibility to ensure that the law provides protection for those who are vulnerable. Similarly social workers who act in loco parentis would have a protective role, as would probation officers and others in the criminal justice system. When we consider teachers or health professionals, however, the issues become less clear. The key question here is whether the role of a teacher, for example, includes the responsibility to try and protect pupils from experiences that the professional considers might be damaging? So, for example, if an individual teacher considers sex outside a stable long-term relationship to be potentially harmful, should he or she include that message as part of the teaching?

A related issue has to do with the setting of boundaries relating to sexual behaviour. This is an area usually considered to be the province of parents, as in whether it is acceptable for a young man or woman to have sex with a partner in the family home. However professionals also have boundaries to consider. Thus teachers will set boundaries when they determine what topics can and cannot be discussed in a sex education class, and they set boundaries when they decide what questions they will answer concerning their own sexual behaviour. Youth workers or social workers will set boundaries when they deem some expressions of sexual behaviour unacceptable in their particular work settings. Too much kissing and fondling in the waiting room may make others feel uncomfortable, and yet laying down strict rules may alienate the very young people the professional wishes to work with.

The role of professional adults in this context involves difficult decisions, and none should pretend there are easy answers. To some extent the individual has to draw on their own values and beliefs, yet these have to be set in the context of the particular work environment. In addition factors such as the legal position in relation to adolescent sexuality have to be considered. Challenges will need to be discussed with colleagues, and support from others is essential. Perhaps most important of all is for the professional to recognise that the role he or she is playing in the context of adolescent sexuality is wider than the particular task of teaching or providing a suitable contraceptive. The professional provides a role model for such things as boundary setting, and the style of communication in relation to intimate or private matters. In addition the values of the professional cannot help but be transmitted to the young person, so sensitivity to the possibility of differing value systems is paramount. Those adults engaged in this field will face challenges not only in the professional but also in the personal domain, and it is for this reason that good training, and a thorough examination of the possible role conflicts inherent in this work, are absolute necessities for all concerned.

2. What do we mean by good sex education?

This question is raised by almost every author contributing to this book. Mitchell (Chapter 6) asks what sort of sex education is needed in today's climate, Moore and Rosenthal (Chapter 3) stress the necessity for open lines of communication between adults and young people, Winn, Roker and Coleman (Chapter 2) query the planning of sex education if we do not consider the knowledge base of the pupils in the first place, Rees, Mellanby and Tripp (Chapter 8) suggest that we look more closely at the role of peers in developing effective sex education, Coyle (Chapter 9) argues for a proactive approach in order to address the needs of gay and lesbian groups, and Thomson and Holland (Chapter 4) urge that a greater emphasis be given to the development of self-confidence and self-worth in sex education programmes.

Throughout the book suggestions are made which bear on the question of what constitutes good sex education. A variety of points are made by the authors, and some attempt will be made here to summarise these. First, it is clear that sex education cannot focus simply on the biology. While biology must be an important component, it is those elements which concern the social context of sexuality, together with relationships and the ethics of sexual behaviour, which are most needed by young people. Teaching the biology of sex is relatively easy, whilst creating a sex education programme which allows young people to explore the dilemmas and contradictions inherent in sexual behaviour, and to develop the necessary relationship skills is very much more difficult. It is in this direction that new thinking in the field should be directed.

A second element of good sex education has to do with the importance of addressing the needs of both young men and young women. This may sound obvious, but it is often overlooked due to the nature of the curriculum, the pressures of timetabling, or indeed to the fact that staff resources for this subject are limited.

As Thomson and Holland (Chapter 4) make very clear sex education rarely addresses the importance of good communication between men and women, nor does it give young people an opportunity to explore the conventional notions of masculinity and feminity. Furthermore the two genders almost certainly need somewhat different things from a good sex education programme.

However there is one thing which both young men and young women need, and that is the space within the curriculum to ask questions and air anxieties in a safe setting. This may involve the creation of single-sex groups for some part of the programme.

A third factor which should be taken into account in the construction of a good sex education programme involves a recognition of the varying levels of knowledge among pupils. This is a point which Winn, Roker and Coleman (Chapter 2) are at pains to emphasize, since it stems from the findings of their recent research on sexual knowledge. The fact is that young people show considerable variation in their knowledge of sexuality. Both age and gender are factors, but equally important is the finding that pupils are more knowledgeable about some topics than about others. As an example young people's knowledge of fertility is relatively poor, in comparison with their knowledge of HIV/AIDS. Such information should inform sex education programmes, and should help teachers to give more attention to the need for evaluation.

A fourth point to emphasise is the one made by Mitchell (Chapter 6) when she asks what kind of sex education we need. Her argument is that we do not need sex education programmes that preempt decisions that young people are likely to make in the realm of sexual behaviour. In other words she does not believe that we should see sex education as being prescriptive, or as giving a "moral message" about what is right and wrong. For Mitchell what constitutes good sex education would be a programme which feeds into the decision-making process, giving young people both skills and knowledge to make informed choices about what is right for them. Of course this is a viewpoint which is not shared by all involved in the field of sex education. In 1997 in the USA enormous amounts of money are being made available by the federal government for programmes which put forward the message that abstinence from sexual intercourse is the right way forward for young people.

Such an approach would not find favour with Mitchell, nor we imagine with many of the authors represented in this book.

Nonetheless the wide divergence of views is one of the reasons why sex education creates such a challenge for those working in the field.

Finally on this question, some note needs to be made of the importance of better training for those who are responsible for sex education programmes. In thinking about what constitutes a good programme we have so far considered the content and the "ethos" or value system associated with the programme. However we should not ignore the fact that any teaching programme is only as good as those who deliver it, and it is a regrettable fact that in most educational systems far too few resources are directed at training and support for those who teach sex education. If we want good programmes we have to recognise that resources must be made available for the professionals who deliver such programmes.

3. What can we do about reducing unwanted teenage pregnancies?

While proportionately very few young women under the age of sixteen become pregnant, the level of social concern about this group is very high indeed. This is particularly true in the USA, which has the highest teenage pregnancy rate in the world, as well as in Britain, which has the highest rate among European countries.

Contained in this book are a number of useful ideas about the prevention of unwanted pregnancies among young women during early and middle adolescence.

The first thing which needs to be said relates to improvements in sex education, and to some extent this has been covered in the discussion above. Sex education has to do more than simply deliver information. The provision of information is important, and without good information it is impossible for young people to make informed choices. Nonetheless sex education cannot stop there. If unwanted pregnancies are to be prevented young women need the skills and self-confidence to negotiate fairly and openly with their partners about sex. If programmes can be constructed so that the personal and relationship issues around sexuality are included, then there will be a better chance that young women will have some control over their fertility.

A second point has to do with the fact that child-bearing must be seen in the context of the role of women in society, rather than as a matter of sexual behaviour only. If young women see opportunities for themselves in the work place, and if they are see that education can make a significant difference to their lives, then they are more likely to be motivated to use contraceptives and to postpone the entry into parenthood. On the other hand where opportunities for fulfilling jobs and useful education do not exist, then motherhood may be a sensible and satisfying choice in the circumstances. As Wellings and Mitchell (Chapter 5) point out, evidence derived from their research shows that low educational attainment and teenage pregnancy are closely related. The more our education system addresses the needs of young women, especially those who are not necessarily high achievers in the conventional sense, the less likely society is to see an increase in the rate of teenage pregnancy.

The incidence of unwanted pregnancy among teenagers is also clearly affected by the level and type of sexual health service available in the locality, a point made by Allen (Chapter 7). From her work in Britain she was able to draw a number of conclusions about the sort of service which would be likely to be most effective. She notes the importance of ensuring that the service is acceptable and welcoming to young men; that it is user-friendly by being accessible and open at times that are appropriate to young people; and that the staff are perceived as sympathetic and trustworthy. There are of course wide differences between countries in the types of sexual health services they provide for young people, and these differences relate to the attitudes and values of the society towards adolescent sexuality. In Holland, for example, where adults are accepting of sexual behaviour among young people, services are readily available, and pregnancy rates are low. In other countries where attitudes are more ambivalent, services for young people are less well resourced and there are generally fewer of them.

To conclude this section we need perhaps to underline the fact that the causes of any teenage pregnancy are complex, and that to target any one element in the overall picture can only make a difference if other factors are also addressed. Thus for example improved sex education has to be coordinated with better access to sexual health services. Even if it were possible to make these two things happen, and this certainly would make a difference, such action still needs to be considered in the context of adult attitudes to teenage sexuality, as well as to educational and employment opportunities for young women. Teenage pregnancy is not only a matter of adolescent sexuality, but it is also an issue of much broader social concern.

4. How can we address the needs of diversity, especially the needs of those who may be gay or lesbian, or of those who come from minority cultures?

We have already referred to the importance of recognising the different needs of young men and young women, and we will return to this theme at the end of the chapter. For a variety of reasons it is often difficult for teachers, as well as for those who develop curricula in the sex education field, to ensure that both male and female perspectives are properly represented, and given the necessary space in discussion and in course work. How much more difficult, therefore, to ensure that gay and lesbian needs are recognised, as well as the needs of those who do not come from the majority culture.

In considering this issue our starting point is the contribution by Coyle (Chapter 9). He makes a number of powerful points in his discussion of sex education, and of its role in allowing gay and lesbian young people to learn about their own sexuality, and to develop a positive identity. Perhaps most telling is his plea for sex education to be proactive in addressing the needs of special groups.

Sex education teachers, hopefully with support from colleagues and researchers, must be willing to stand up against established opinion, whether it originates from politicians, from school governors, or from parents, and argue for the inclusion of certain topics in the curriculum, even if these are controversial. The exploration of issues surrounding homosexuality is one such example.

Another perspective on this has to do with the style of teaching. For many, a free and open approach to discussion in sex education is preferable. If teachers take an approach which allows the students to determine subjects for discussion, and offers them a relatively free rein, this is often considered to be very positive. By using such a style adults can show that they are able to relinquish control of the agenda, and it is assumed that this will provide opportunities for common concerns and anxieties to be raised. There is, however, a danger with such an approach, since young people themselves will have topics which they may prefer to avoid. One of these may very well be gay and lesbian sex. It is essential, therefore, that teachers and others involved in sex education have clear goals in respect of the topics that need to be covered. Young people will need direction and guidance in order to deal with the more sensitive issues, and it is here that professional adults can play such an important role.

Whilst considering the role of adults it is worth noting a further point in relation to the needs of gay and lesbian young people, and of those from minority cultures. The needs of these groups cannot be addressed unless such young people feel safe from prejudice and the possibility of harassment, whether of a racist or sexist nature. To create such a safe environment must be the responsibility of the professional adult; a responsibility which links with our earlier discussion of the necessity for the adult to set boundaries with respect to sexual behaviour. Adults also need to set boundaries in relation to social behaviour, and one key area here has to do with prejudice. Some adults may say that much of this behaviour is outside their control. They should think again. Adults represent powerful role models, and their own behaviour relating to sexism and racism will be very influential in determining the climate of the classroom or group. In addition, as we have indicated, adults can be proactive in determining whether, and how, certain topics are covered in the curriculum. Finally they can work to create open, accepting environments in their school, youth group or institution, so that those who feel different are assured that they are safe and that their beliefs, their culture, or their sexuality is accepted by the majority.

5. What do we know about effective services for young people?

Allen's chapter (Chapter 7) is an essential starting point for any consideration of this issue, since her research illustrates some of the key principles relating to sexual health services for young people. Some reference has already been made to this issue in our discussion of teenage pregnancy. In one sense effective services for young people will be no different from effective services for all ages. However there are some problems which are particular to service provision for the adolescent population, many of which stem from the complex and often ambivalent attitudes of the adults involved in providing such services.

In considering effective services the problem of ambiguity, or ambivalence, is a good place to start. To take an example, in one southern county of Britain they are proud of their sexual health advice service for young people. The opening hours are from 2 to 4 p.m. on two afternoons a week. When it is pointed out that this is hardly the most convenient time for those who are at school or at work, the response is that this is the only time it is possible to staff the service. This sort of ambiguity is common, although it is expressed in many different ways. On the one hand adults acknowledge the need for special services, yet on the other they may make such services difficult to access, through timing, geographical location, failure to advertise, or through inappropriate staffing. If sexual health services are to be effective, and if they are to meet the needs of young people, then one thing which is essential is for commitment on the part of the adults involved.

Confidentiality is another element which needs to be addressed. Research makes it clear that one of the factors most likely to discourage young people from using a service is if they believe that confidentiality will be breached, and that their parents may be informed of their visit to the centre or clinic. Of especial importance here is the role of the receptionist or person answering the telephone. The first contact point is crucial, and the response the young person receives to his or her enquiry is likely to determine whether the service is seen as appropriate. It is through this first contact that the young person will rate the attitude of the service, and in particular he or she will be assessing whether adults are likely to be sympathetic or judgemental, patronising or accepting. A service which seeks to be effective with young people will pay as much attention to the first point of contact as to all the other professional tasks involved.

Finally an effective service is one which takes into account the needs of both young men and young women. All too frequently it is the needs of young women which are seen as being of first importance, and there are often good and pressing reasons why this should be so. However unless male partners can feel that they are a part of the consultation process, whether this concerns contraception or any other aspect of sexual behaviour, the chances of the consultation being of value are considerably lessened. Furthermore men too need advice and support, even if they themselves are not the ones who may become pregnant. Allen's research made it clear that there are many ways in which services actually discourage the involvement of men, through their publicity, their image in the community, the attitudes of staff, or even through the lack of a suitable waiting area. If attention can be given to factors such as these, and a real effort made to ensure that a male viewpoint is considered, it is undoubtedly possible to create services which do meet the needs of both genders.

6. *How can we recognise the differing needs of young men and young women in relation to sex education?*

This question follows on from the previous discussion, and many of the points to be made have implications for the provision of services. Nonetheless there are very particular issues which underlie the nature and format of sex education programmes, and it is to these that we will now turn. First, if we are to recognise the differing needs of the two genders, it is essential for adults to acknowledge that there are different pressures on men and women which impact on their sexual behaviour. This is a point made by both Moore and Rosenthal (Chapter 3) as well as by Thomson and Holland (Chapter 4). As all these authors emphasize, sex takes place within a social context, and the norms and values of male and female peer groups are different. For varying and complex reasons pressures on women may act to minimize or to underplay sexual behaviour, whilst for men there may be pressure to exaggerate or to boast of sexual activity. In addition to this the personal and psychological needs of men and women vary, a fact which may also lead to differences of interpretation and meaning.

It is this dimension of the social and emotional meaning of sex that is critical for the construction of sex education which is pertinent and appropriate to both genders. Sex does carry different meanings for males and females in our society, and therefore unless we make it possible for young people to explore both sets of meanings in our sex education programmes then one or other group will be at a disadvantage. In this respect it may be worth noting that programmes which really meet the needs of both genders need to pay particular attention to matters of equality and power in sexual relationships. Teachers should work towards creating a climate in the classroom which ensures as much equality as possible, since it is in modelling the relationship between men and women that teachers and others who work in this field can do most to influence the type of relationship which exists in an intimate, sexual context.

The role of the peer group in delivering some aspects of sex education may also be of significance here. As Rees, Mellanby and Tripp (Chapter 8) show, teenagers can play a significant part in programmes as peer tutors or peer educators, and in this context teachers can ensure that both young men and young women have equal roles. In an ideal world it would be possible for a man and a woman to act as joint teachers in sex education programmes, but since this is rarely an option, another way to ensure that the male and female perspectives are represented is to use young people themselves, and to allow them to model good communication and to show how power and control can be shared in the classroom.

To conclude, there has been an emphasis throughout this chapter on the need to have equality as a central tenet in any sex education programme, or indeed in any service provision. Where sexuality is the focus of work with young people, then an integral aspect of that work should be a commitment to the needs of both genders. It is only through such a commitment that we can expect to enable young people to have more satisfying and worthwhile sexual relationships. It is towards this goal that sex education and sexual health services should be directed.

Resources Section: Organisations and Further Reading

Organisations

Association for Lesbian, Gay and Bisexual Psychologies UK (ALGBP-UK): P O Box 7534, London, NW1 0ZA. (To obtain a list of lesbian and gay affirmative therapists, send an SAE to this address).
Brook Advisory Centres (National Office): 165 Grays Inn Road, London, WC1X 8UD. Tel. 0171 713 9000. (Helpline number 0171 617 8000).
Family Planning Association: 2–12 Pentonville Road, London, N19FP. Tel. 0171 837 5432. (Helpline number 0171 837 4044).
London Lesbian and Gay Switchboard: 0171 837 7324.
National Friend: BM National Friend, London, WC1N 3XX.
Sex Education Forum: c/o NCB, 8 Wakley Street, London, EC1V 7QE. Tel 0171 843 6052/6051.

Further reading/References

Coleman, J. (1995), *Teenagers and Sexuality*. London: Hodder Headline.

Gullotta, T., Adams, R. and Montemayor, R. (1994), *Adolescent Sexuality*. London: Sage.

Heaven, P. (1996), *Adolescent Health*. London: Routledge.

Johnson, A., Wadsworth, J., Wellings, K. and Field, J. (1994), *Sexual Attitudes and Lifestyles*. London: Blackwell.

Madaras, L. (1989), *What's Happening To My Body?: A growing-up guide for parents and sons*. London: Penguin.

Moore, S. and Rosenthal, D. (1993), *Sexuality in Adolescence*. London: Routledge.

Moore, S., Rosenthal, D. and Mitchell, A. (1996), *Youth, AIDS and Sexually Transmitted Diseases*. London: Routledge.

Plant, M. and Plant, M. (1992), *Risk-Takers: Alcohol, Drugs, Sex and Youth*. London: Routledge.

Stoppard, M. (1992), *Everygirl's Lifeguide*. London: Dorling Kindersley.

INDEX